THE CITY COUNCIL IS YOUR WORST ENEMY

THE CITY COUNCIL IS YOUR WORST ENEMY

A CHAOTIC LIFE IN CHARLOTTESVILLE

STANTON BRAVERMAN

To order additional copies of this book, contact:
Xlibris
1-888-795-4274
www.Xlibris.com
Orders@Xlibris.com
798954

In memory of Jennifer Braverman

CONTENTS

CHAPTER 1

HOW DID I GET HERE?

IT IS NOT clear exactly how we ended up in this town. A person can make mistakes and being here is one of them. Over the years I have lived in many cities and towns and got along well with the local government. That includes inner city Washington DC when Marion Barry was mayor. Once I got here there was no choice but to declare war on the City Council.

It is a well-known small town about 120 miles south of Washington DC. The University of Virginia is there as well as a major medical center that is part of the university. But there was something about it that told me to stay away. Years ago there were things about the place that just did not mesh with who I was. It was known as a place where many of the people were haughty. The conversations were about Polo Pony events, the Fox Hunts, who was rich and important. They were not well liked by many Washingtonians. It was a place with a major university where the students were relatively quiet during the massive protests against the Vietnam War and the Civil Rights Movement, which were going on while I was in law school.

In the 1960s and 1970s Washington DC was dynamic. So much was happening there. The eyes of the world were focused on it. In 1966, when I first got there, with a job as an International Economist at the US Treasury I met up with thousands of young people such as myself, professionals who were determined to do something to help America. We were the generation that heard John F. Kennedy tell us to "ask not what our country can do for us. Ask what we can do for our country." We heard and we believed it.

For years my world was with the peasants, a love of the masses, of hard working people who were close to their families and cared for their neighbors. Life started in South Philadelphia, the streets that Rocky Balboa would run through as he trained for his next major fight. University life was Temple while living at home, working to pay for tuition. There were no university football games, no fancy parties, just a lost kid trying to find his way in the world. As an undergraduate, my major was Finance. There was something that was intriguing about money: what it was, how it got its value and how people earned it. But to a Jewish kid in Philly in the 1960s with the local banks controlled by the Upper Class (or the Blue Bloods as Dad always labeled them), there was no room for a Jew. It was an accepted fact of life that we were told by the local Jewish community and I did not believe it until I graduated and applied for a job at a bank. They were honest and confirmed that Jews were not wanted.

In a way, that was probably the best thing that happened to me. It meant going back to the university at night for an MBA and a job as a long term substitute teacher at a rough high school in the worst section of the city. This time my focus was International Finance, exchange rates, and international financial institutions. It was dull stuff to most people but I loved it. That led to a job at the Treasury and working in Washington DC. That was a great job where I learned more about finance and economics than from all of the 60 plus economic credits from two degrees. The job taught a young student how to write and think; the kid from Philly found himself. But I needed more. It was time to reach out to other worlds and it lead to enrollment at American University law school at night. My expectation was that law would be an adjunct to economics but after falling in love with law, it was economics that was the adjunct to a new career as an attorney.

Washington has more lawyers per capita than any other city in the world. And many of them are looking for work. I needed to find a shortcut to a law career and that was to open my own office; after all, the fastest way to become a senior partner in a law firm is to start your own. My first office was two small rooms across the street from the Treasury where I continued to work on a part time basis. My secretary was the answering machine. There was an unlisted telephone number, a desk and me. About a month later a man walked in and said he needed an

STANTON BRAVERMAN

attorney and I replied, "This is our lucky day, because I need a client." and from there it was one client after another and it was great to be the boss, to get a reputation for being a good attorney and to make enough money to feed the family, provide for the kids' education and to put a roof over their heads.

At times when I think back to the job interview in Philly at the bank and being told that they are not hiring Jews, I wish I could thank them for doing what they did because it pushed me onto better and more interesting things. Had they given me the job, 40 years later I would probably be sitting at the same desk.

The years quickly went by. Being an attorney was far more exciting than being an international economist and before I knew it, it was time to retire; we sold the house in Arlington and moved out to the mountain cabin, a quiet place in Madison county, surrounded by the Shenandoah National Park where there were more bears than people. It was great living there, but it could get boring or lonely or there was a need to be around more people. This led to buying a house in Charlottesville Virginia: a town that many years before was a bypass zone, a place that did not interest me. But it was only 40 miles south of the cabin; after going there for groceries and observing what seemed to be significant changes, we decided to try it. At first we intended to live there and use the cabin as a weekend retreat. But it was financed from the proceeds of the sale of a rental house and the CPA advised that we had to rent it or pay a huge tax bill. That took us by surprise and the house was rented and we just stayed as full time residents at the cabin. The real home was in the mountains and the Charlottesville house would have been a place to go to when there was a need for the chaos of city life. And all through this journey from Philly to Cville, life seemed to go my way. And even Cville was acceptable; in many ways it's still acceptable, except for the need to declare war on the local government. This book is about this war, how I fought it and why it was necessary to be so aggressive.

CHAPTER 2

WHO AM I?

MOST PEOPLE ARE not inclined to be aggressive. They are trained to be quiet, to remain calm and if there is a problem, they should hold the anger back and slowly let it out. But any person who started life in South Philadelphia, taught high school at a rough inner-city ghetto school and spent four decades representing demanding immigrants from almost every country in the world has lost any skills in being so well mannered. There would be arguments with clients, government officials, neighbors, friends and family. We would tell it as it is. Then after the storm, it was time to laugh, tell jokes and convey the fact that we cared for each other. One friend, who was from the "well-mannered school" cried when I yelled at him. He did not know how to deal with it. "You must hate me," he said as he wiped back the tears. But that was not true because it take a lot of effort to yell at someone. I told him that in a strange way it means I care for him and was willing to invest so much energy into the conversation. After our tempers cooled down we remained friends.

One day at the office a Chinese client wanted me to prepare a visa application that included fraudulent statements. I refused to prepare the application the way he wanted it done and told him that it was illegal to make a false statement to the government. The false statement dealt with an issue which, while he thought it to be important, had no relationship to the petition and did not have to be made. When he insisted that it be done his way I would not agree with him. At that time I was taking prednisone because of a medical problem which made me rather irritable. The client got angry and grabbed his file from my desk and started running to the door. I got up, chased him into the corridor about four feet from the office door, tackled him and we were scuffing at each other. After we both calmed down he agreed to do it my way. The documents were filed and his adjustment of status application was quickly approved. We then talked about the incident and by then he realized that his need to make a false statement would not have worked out. After the adjustment interview we started to joke about the fight. He started off by saying, "I got scared. I saw you as a John Wayne type character that would kick the shit out of me."

Then I replied, "That is funny because I saw you as a Bruce Lee fighter who was about to give me a karate chop that would leave me in a wheelchair for the rest of my life. We laughed, shook hands and agreed to keep in contact.

Reading stories of how aggressive I was at times would convince the reader that I was a mad man. That was true only some of the time. Mostly I was a quiet person who got along with other people except when I perceived them as trying to pull a fast one on me. As Jennifer would tell people, my temperament could go from zero to sixty in a split second. While such behavior at times scared people it was a great attribute for being an immigration attorney. And it was this part of my personality that carried me through the war with the City Council.

CHAPTER 3

THE LAW OFFICE

AFTER OPENING THE first law office and working on a variety of legal issues – divorces, contracts, personal injury, etc. - I quickly realized that a single attorney could not run a general practice law firm It was just too much work and there was a need to focus on one type of law. Specialization of labor is the secret to the industrial revolution and it was time to go in that direction. Within a month after opening the office I starting working on a number of immigration issues. It was an area of law that was slowly emerging; there were only five other attorneys in the city who had any real knowledge of this issue. Most other lawyers thought that an immigration law was a joke and often refused to acknowledge that is was real legal work and not something that could be done by a paralegal. Often, other attorneys would comment that all an immigration lawyer did was walk around the immigration service with a bag of money and hand it out to government officials as a way of getting green cards for clients. This was in the early 1980s when the immigration laws were quite generous. It was not illegal to hire an undocumented worker; they could easily get social security cards and driver's licenses. It was a time when an employer could hire and train an employee for a job and then sponsor the immigrant. There was an annual meeting of the American Immigration and Naturalization Attorneys, with the acronym of AINL. Two hundred attorneys from the private bar and about 100 government officials would meet to discuss the emerging area of law that was so new of a field of study that there was almost no literature on the subject. The participants spent hours telling stories and trading secrets on how the immigration system worked. There were not many immigrants in the country at that time but their numbers were quickly growing. The

Immigration law group, which consisted of attorneys and government officials who worked with immigration issues, became close friends. It was similar to being in a huge family that would meet each year. The annual meeting was a family reunion where government officials and the private bar would come together.

My law office opened in 1972, the year I passed the Bar Examination, the year I left my job at the Treasury Department. Because there was a shortage of immigration attorneys the practice grew and there was a huge assortment of immigrants who needed legal advice. At first the clients were maids and cooks, then auto mechanics and construction workers. These were the type of folks that I enjoyed working for. But soon the clientele went upscale and there were foreign research scientists and medical doctors and university professors and employees of international organizations. One moment I would be on the phone talking to a housewife who hired a maid and governess for her family. That would be followed by a phone conversation with a medical doctor and the hospital administration that wanted to employ him. And that conversation followed by another telephone conversation with a major research company that needed to hire a foreign scientist to assist in a secret government project; what the research about was something I was not allowed to know. I could list a number of major corporations who had retained me to help with their employees. The immigrants and the employers were exciting and interesting people to work with. Many of the immigrants were poor and glad to find jobs and many of the employers needed the immigrants. The best part was the practice made a nice income while most of the Bar thought that immigrants could not afford a lawyer. My work was to help people secure their lives, find jobs and feed their children.

This was the most exciting period of my life. Law school, a marriage that turned sour and a job that I got tired of were behind me. The drive was not for money, but rather to be whatever I wanted to be. In a way it was a secret world. There was no competition from other lawyers because they all believed that immigrants could not pay a legal fee (which clearly was not true.) There was no interest by other lawyers in being part of the group, especially a group with the acronym of AINL.

Being my own boss, I could do what I wanted to do. I could pick and choose clients, I could determine the hours and days of the week the office would be open and when I made a decision about how to handle a complicated legal matter, it was my decision and there was not a senior person near me to veto the action. At times my decisions were based on my low level of insanity which surprisingly worked in my favor. For example, when I opened the office I attempted to have a listing in the telephone book. After all, in 1972 every attorney has his or her name listed. While talking to the phone company about this listing, I was told that there was only a free listing for the Washington D.C. phone book; to be listed in the Northern Virginia and Maryland phone books, even though they were the same metropolitan area, would cost a lot of money. Yet to be listed in only the Washington DC phone book would reach out to only a small part of the local community. It was ridiculous and it was the telephone company's way of ripping off the local business community. To a 1960s hippy it was unconscionable. Just before I slammed down the instrument, I told the telephone company to just make it an unlisted telephone number, not to list the phone number anywhere, which did not cost anything. Other lawyers laughed when they found out about this - the office phone was an unlisted number. They said I was crazy because the listing in the phone book was the only way to get new clients. "Braverman, you are crazy" but I stuck to my decision and soon this worked to my advantage. Clients, when in the office, would take with them a number of my business cards. They would give them out to their friends and tell them that this lawyer is so good his name is not in the telephone book. As my father taught me years ago, every successful business got started because of a successful gimmick. There had to be something to make the business different from the competitors and my gimmick, for the moment, was the fact that the office was the only law firm in Washington DC that was not listed in the phone book.

CHAPTER 4

THE LAW OFFICE AND CHARLOTTESVILLE

THE PERCEPTION OF immigration law started to change by 1980. About that time both the Washington Post and the New York Times wrote articles that told the public that immigration lawyers were making money. That got almost every law firm in America interested in the influx of immigrants and by 1985 it became known as the law for the future. Clients were from every country and they lived throughout the United States. It was a time when America woke up to the skills those immigrants had to offer the country. The employers were anxious to assist, to find out if there was something they could to do to help. That was true everywhere except in one town and that was Charlottesville. Whenever an employer from there would call, it always left me with the nagging feeling that that employer was more interested in exploiting the immigrant than helping and the call was often nothing more than a front to convince the immigrant that they were seriously concerned about their immigrant status. And almost every time my feeling turned out to be correct because the employer would refuse to fully cooperate. Often when the immigrant came to my office to find out if the employer was cooperative my advice was to find another job outside of that town.

I just could not fully understand why I did not like the town. Maybe it was the upper class rich southern white Anglo-Saxon society that reminded me of the bank officer who interviewed me. It could be that my attitude toward the people in the town could be felt by them in the limited conversations and they just did not like me. Whatever the case, I did not like the place.

Being a socialist at heart may be the problem. Representing the cooks, maids, and mechanics was not what most Charlottesville attorneys saw as a successful practice. The law work was also so much different from the work at the Treasury where I had little contact with real people and saw the world through statistics and numbers generated through an IBM 1400. . The world came into being from the mud and water around us and it grew into what it is today. That is the way the world progressed. It starts with supporting basic humanity and it was highly rewarding. Consider the maids. They worked so hard, they paid their taxes; they raised a number of American children while their parents worked and they never got arrested for anything. To me they were important people and I treated them with kindness and understanding.

Immigrant maids like to talk or gossip with each other. And they would often talk about the immigration lawyer who was working on their green card. They would pass around my name and one of my many business cards to a friend who in turn would pass it on someone else. They would ask their employer for help in getting a legal status in the country and they would give my card to the employer with a request that they call me. It was amazing how the word spread around the country and the different immigrant groups, especially since my name was not in the telephone books. Calls came in from California, or from overseas, from New York, Atlanta, Canada and every corner in the world and they were all pleasant and interesting people to work with except when the call came from Charlottesville. Many of the employers were highly educated and leading people in the country. Most of the time they knew nothing about immigration and when speaking to me would ask basic questions about how the immigration process worked. Many times, a person had questions about hiring a governess for her children. Other times the person on the phone was at work and an immigration problem arose, such as hiring a foreign trained engineer who had technology that the company needed; they would call me for advice. The person got my name from their nanny and soon the company and the engineer would be a client. Or they may call back because someone they knew had a relative who wanted to immigrate to

     STANTON BRAVERMAN

the US. At that time there was not a significant number of Americans who were anti-immigrant because there were not many immigrants in the country. It was exciting times for a born again hippie from the 1960s, except when the cases came from Charlottesville.

One day a major French international company called my office and requested that I immediately come to their US headquarters to discuss an important immigration issue. The office was in Maryland, about an hour from my office. It turned out that the CEO of US operations was denied a visa by the US embassy in Paris. When I got there everyone was upset. Some of the staff thought it was a reflection of anti-French attitude by the US government at the time. After reviewing the documents it turned out that the CEO has asked for the wrong visa classification. He had asked for an L-1 visa and should have asked for an E-2 visa. I advised them to put the check mark into a different spot and re-apply. It was easy money. We then went to lunch and I was curious to know how they got my telephone number; they told me that it was another nanny referral. I had represented the nanny's girlfriend. The officer had in her hand the card that had been passed around. It looked like a worn out one dollar bill. I giggled to myself while I gave her a couple of my new cards hoping she would pass them along to other companies with whom they did business. (The next day the company called the office to say the visa was issued and all was well.) That started a long-term relationship with a French company and -yes – the cards were passed to other European companies who had operations in the US.

I would be slow in responding to calls that came in from employers in Charlottesville because I just did not believe that they were serious clients and that the American employer was not really interested in helping the immigrant. This came through because they often just did not ask the same questions that the other employers asked. They did not want to know how long the immigration process would take or what were their legal responsibilities or how much experience did I have. They just acted as if they were really not that interested in the matter.

Thinking back about the law practice and Charlottesville I remember one case from the city. It did not start as a Charlottesville case but ended up being from there. It was a young woman from Europe who was about 22 years old, rather pretty but clearly overweight and in need of losing somewhat more than a few pounds. She got a job as a nanny for a well-off family in the DC area and I was retained to assist her in applying for permanent resident status. The young woman was well dressed and made a nice appearance and was excited to get the job. After meeting her and the employer in the office, the paper work went along fine and I would periodically call the employer to see how the employment arrangement worked out. The employer told me that the young woman was so responsible that they bought a car for her to use and as I was about to hang up they asked if it was OK for them to get her a membership in a local health club. I assured them it would not be a problem.

About a year later I looked into my appointment book and noticed that the young lady was scheduled to meet with me. As far as I was concerned, there was no reason to meet but the office still gave her an appointment. About an hour later the staff told me that she was in the waiting room and I went out to greet her. And there in front of me was a young lady who was movie star beautiful with a body that most movie stars would beg for. I looked at her and asked who she was and it turned out she was the same pudgy young lady who was previously in my office. I apologized for not recognizing her and she then came into the office for a consultation.

"I am getting married," she told me. It turns out the family she worked for was concerned about her being overweight and they sent her to the health club on a daily basis. It was there that she met her fiancée. He was a young attorney from Charlottesville; he had a nice job and his family was well connected in the community. The client married the young man and then moved to Charlottesville. About a year and a half later she was back in the office asking about her immigration status in light of the fact that she was now separated from her husband and planning to get a divorce as quickly as possible. I assured her that her status would still be valid and asked why what seemed to be a happy relationship went bad so quickly. She replied, "It is the way of life in the town. Everyone is trying to outdo the other person; it is a game where the richest person wins. There would be parties and lot of drinking, horse events I had to go to, and everyone is trying to outdo the other person. I just could not take it anymore. She got her divorce, kept her green card and I did not hear from her again for a couple more years when she came into the office to ask about applying for US citizenship. She told me she got remarried to a local high school teacher; they bought a small house in a nice neighborhood and were planning to have a couple of kids. When I asked her about her life in Charlottesville she snarled and said it was one of life's mistakes.

About the time she got her divorce two young ladies, also from Europe, were professionals and were traveling through the United States as tourists. They visited Charlottesville and told me that they loved the town and were interested in resettling there; they thought surely they could find quality bachelors to marry. I told them to go do that if that is what they wanted. About eight months later they were back in my office to tell me that they were returning to Europe and giving up the idea of finding a husband in that town. I asked what the problem was and they went on and on about the spoiled rich men that lived there and they just did not like the way of life the city had to offer.

One day a Mexican immigrant was in the office about his immigration status. He had entered illegally and was working as a farm hand in the Charlottesville area. He wanted to marry a local woman but needed to first get a divorce from his current wife who he had not lived with for many years. He lived in Charlottesville long enough to qualify as a resident of the state for applying for a divorce.

but he could not find a lawyer in the area who would represent him. They all said that illegal aliens had no rights. I then tried to contact a lawyer in the area to advise that they could handle a divorce and was unsuccessful. The lawyers I spoke to did not want the money and they did not want to deal with an immigrant farm worker. But there was an easy solution and that was a lawyer in Northern Virginia who would handle it. His fee was $500. The client went over to his office, signed some papers and two weeks later he was divorced. It was an easy divorce, easy money and I could not understand why an attorney in Charlottesville would turn it down.

These two cases confirmed my feeling that Charlottesville was a town to stay away from. But at the same time I have many friends who graduated from the University of Virginia and they all love the town. Many of them have told me that they are jealous that when I retired I ended up living there and they are not. Each year the University graduates a large number of students; many of them then try to find a way to continue living there. Charlottesville became their new home and they just wanted to stay. But I never attended the university, I was not part of that section of the town and I saw the town from a different angle. In effect there is a lot more to the town than just the university.

I tend to be "politically incorrect" and will often say things that often that are not socially condoned. One friend once described me as an intelligent person who can hold a great conversation and tell interesting stories, but whatever happens, do not cut me loose at a diplomatic reception. This is not entirely true because there were many official functions that I successfully attended when working at the Treasury. In fact, in Geneva, during a plenary meeting of the United Nations Council for Trade and Development the US Mission hosted a diplomatic lunch for me to meet many of the representatives from some of the member countries. But that was years ago and today I would agree with the comment. For example, one day a woman from the Charlottesville area called to ask if I could represent her newly hired, undocumented housekeeper from Mexico. It may have been the tone in her voice that was best described as "Charlottesville Haughtiness" or it was the fact that at that moment I was rather burned out with cases going bad in that town and I said, "Oh just what I need: Another mother from Charlottesville who does not want to raise her children." About three seconds afterwards the woman abruptly hung up the phone. In a way I was hoping my rudeness would discourage other employers in the town from calling me.

Now Charlottesville was not the only haughty community in Virginia. There are others, but these employers, while they may be difficult, did treat their staff with respect. I remember one interesting case where a maid had worked for a rather wealthy employer in Great Falls Maryland for well over ten years. She came to the office to ask if

     STANTON BRAVERMAN

she could get a green card and had with her a folder full of documents that she then handed to me. Inside the folder was a ten year old approved Alien Labor Certification that has been submitted for her by the employer. Neither the employer nor the immigrant was in a hurry to complete the immigration process. I looked at the labor document and noted that it showed the salary to be $80 a week, plus free room and board. That was the wage from the prior decade, but the agency regulations were such that it still applied. I asked the maid what she was getting paid and she said $80 a week. The office prepared the necessary documents for the application for permanent residence and filed it with the Immigration Service in Baltimore. About six months later I was with her in Baltimore for the final interview. The Examiner looked at the documents, looked at the salary, and the current letter by the employer that stated that she had been and was still receiving $80 a week. The Examiner clearly understood that it was an approvable document but he just did not like it because he felt the maid was being abused. He asked her if she intended to find another job once she got her green card – a job that would be paying more money - and the Maid, replied "No" Then he asked why did she not want to work for more money and a tear came into her eye. "I love the children, they are like mine. In addition, they take good care of me. If I get sick they pay the doctor bill, if I need new clothes they buy them for me. When they go on vacation I go with them. I am part of the family and $80 a week is more than I need." The examiner looked at me and commented. "Nice job, Braverman; I wish all your cases were as nice as this one." Nothing like this, that I know of, ever happened in Charlottesville.

However, in 1996 things seemed to turn around in that town and the few new cases went rather smoothly and the employers impressed me on how well they treated the employees. A major country club that hired a number of Mexicans wanted to know if they could hire an English teacher to help the Mexican employees with their English. The local police department started to give Spanish language lessons to the police officers. It seemed that stogie Charlottesville was coming of age. In many ways it was an interesting town. The University of Virginia and its huge medical complex dominates the city, the culture and the economy.

The city is only 45,000 people and when the university football game is at the home field it will hold well over that number of people. The hospital employs many doctors, hospital personnel, nurses and other staff. The one hour rush hour at 5:00 is the outpouring of employees from the hospital. At the current time the city and county are about 150,000 people. But the general population is well-off and for a small town there are a significant number of high end expensive gourmet food markets. There is a Trader Joe's, a Whole Foods, three Kroger's, two Harris Teeters, one Giant, and a number of Food Lions. A Wagman's is under construction along with a Costco. And finally a Walmart and Sam's Club are there. There are a large number of restaurants that serve all types of American and ethnic foods. There are theaters for plays and orchestras, extensive libraries, a fantastic downtown section without auto traffic where people from all walks of life promenade from one restaurant to another. For a small town, there is always something to do and it is never boring.

But to give the reader more of an explanation on how I got here. I grew up in a Jewish ghetto in Philadelphia in the 1950s. This was a community of second generation immigrants who believed that by coming to America they were all rich, It was a community that in the process of becoming Americanized focused on the value structure of their first generation parents which was the three Es: education, education and education. But my dream as a kid, influenced by TV shows and cowboy movies, was to escape the city life and live on a farm. The year I married Jennifer (1979) I realized that the law office was very stressful and there was a need to find someplace to break the stress level and my hope was that a place in the country would allow for me to kick off a lot of the stress. While stress has been identified as the cause of many illnesses, a human can deal with high levels of stress providing there is a place or way to duck it for a while. We started looking for such a place. One choice was to buy a house near the ocean with a quiet beach. But most beach communities are very crowded during the summer months and Jennifer, who is a very light-skinned blonde, was not a sun worshiper. And besides, it was not my dream town. We needed something different. That led us to Claiborne, a small

     STANTON BRAVERMAN

fishing village on the Eastern Shore of the Chesapeake Bay outside of St. Michaels, Maryland. It was a community of about 30 homes where most of the locals were fishermen or, as the locals call themselves, "Watermen". They earned their living off of the bay by crabbing in the summer, oysters in the winter, eels in the spring, hunting guides in the winter. We bought an old house/store on the main street to use as a weekend retreat. When we moved in and met the locals they were nice and friendly but concerned that a Jewish lawyer from Washington DC would really never become a member of the community and his two sons would probably not fit in with the local kids. But soon we were part of the community and Danny and Kenny developed close relationships with all of the local kids. It was a great place. We worked on remodeling the house, planted a huge veggie garden in the backyard that overlooked the bay, It was a great place to bike ride. This was my first exposure to a culture that is popularly known as redneck. Their lives were not focused on getting any more education than needed to earn a living, they were religious and they were willing to help each other with many day to day chores and needs. Four miles away was St Michaels, Maryland which was a town of about 1500 people with a hardware store, a drug store and a supermarket and a local bar and a restaurant to cater to the tourists who mostly arrive by sailboat from Annapolis, which was across the bay.

"We all" just loved the town as the local culture and language started to influence us. But like all great places, time slowly changes them. It was soon discovered when the Washington Post and the New York Times wrote articles about the local charm. (Again the Post and Times are disrupting my life) Also, the book, Magnificent Swimmers, which was about the life of the bay and the crabbing industry, won a Pulitzer Prize and was read by every intellectual in the Eastern part of the US. Slowly the tourists bought houses, some retired here, and it became the "in" place to be. One of the local mansions outside of St. Michaels was a place where Jennifer and I would meet the locals at night, get a pitcher of beer and then throw darts at a dart board. It was bought by Laura Ashley and turned into a five star luxury bed and breakfast. Once it was opened the locals were told to stay away. As the community changed the locals moved away and city folk, who I was running away from, took over everything. When we first got there the town tourist industry closed down by Thanksgiving. Within ten years, the town stayed open all year and expensive restaurants were opening up on Main Street. One day we found out that Dick Cheney and Donald Rumsfeld bought property in the area and we knew it was time to move on. We rented out the house and moved back on a full time basis to Arlington VA and decided to try to find a similar type of town, but this time in the Shenandoah mountains that were about 80 miles West of the DC area.

In 1990 we bought a fantastic piece of land that was adjacent to the wilderness of the Shenandoah National Park that had a magnificent view of Old Rag Mountain. It was 29 acres and an old house that needed to be taken down. It was 84 miles from the office and 40 miles north of Charlottesville. After buying the property our plan was to take down the old house and build a new cabin that would be for weekends.

It took us a year of traveling all over mountains of Virginia, Maryland and West Virginia to find this property. On weekends there would be exploration west of DC and other times it would be north. Surrounding the DC area, beginning about 60 miles away are a number of mountains that are part of the Appalachian chain that runs from Vermont to Georgia. Every so often there would be an interesting house for sale and when asked why it is for sale the answer was either "The husband loves it, the wife hates it and they are now divorced," or it would be "Wife loves it, husband hates it and they are now divorced." Since I am very much in love with my wife, it was important that Jennifer be overly excited about any property we would buy. There were many failures. After seeing a number of interesting houses and mini farms that fit our budget which Jennifer vetoed, the search looked like it would never work out and I was fearful that the family would be stuck inside the beltway for an eternity. Now Jennifer is a WASP from a debutante society and I am a pushy Jewish kid from inner city Philadelphia. I wear all of my emotions on my sleeve and she seems to generally hold them back. When I get angry I get excited and will get loud. When she gets angry she will clam up or start to cry which gets me even more upset. What is interesting, we are from two different planets but we seem to be able to communicate. In the end she gets what she wants though Jennifer will strongly disagree with this statement and points out that there many things I got that she did not want, such as the $70,000 RV I bought that was a total disaster. But, as Jennifer politely says "My husband is good at laying down the law and I then do as I damn well please."

One summer day we were in Madison County, five miles north of the town of Syria and looking at a 29 acre lot that was adjacent to the national forest. The only way to describe on how to get there is to go down a small country road along the Robinson River, cross over a couple of one lane wooden bridges. When you get close to the property the road turns into a one lane road that handles traffic going in both directions. Since few people use the road then there is seldom a problem with oncoming cars. About a half mile later you turn on to a rutted dirt road and go about 1000 feet, ford the river and then up a rutted dirt mountain road. Another way to describe it is to tell people that when they say to themselves "Where the hell am I?" you know you are almost there.

There was an old house that clearly had to come down. There were snake skins on the floor of the porch. It was vacant. It did not have running water, electricity or a septic field. Jennifer got out of the car, carefully walked through the house, got on the old porch, kicked away a couple of snake skins and said, "interesting" which in WASP talk means "This place is great, lets buy it." It was a lot more than what I wanted to pay for a house in the mountains. But then again, it was cheaper than the cost of a divorce.

CHAPTER 5

REAL ESTATE IN CVILLE

FOR A NUMBER of years my hobby was to remodel old homes. In 1972 I remodeled a home on Swann Street in Washington DC that I bought for $30,000. A few years later we bought the house in Claiborne, Maryland, just outside of St. Michaels for $35,000. In 1986 I bought a house in Arlington for $175,000 (paid for from the profits of the sale of the house on Swann Street). Each house was remodeled and I was quite sure I had the skills to build a cabin in the mountains. Over the years I learned carpentry, electrical circuits, tiling, dry walling, putting up siding, painting and some plumbing. (Plumbing and I just do not get along.) The cabin turned out to be an enjoyable two year project and in the end the family had an incredible weekend property in the middle of a wilderness. By 1993 the house was finished, by 1996 the pond was done, by 1999 the guest house was done and it was time to sit back and totally relax while there. Everyone in the family fell in love with Madison County and the locals and the simple ways of life. They were basically the same people and culture that we enjoyed being with in the early days in Claiborne but they earned their income from the mountains. At that time the population of the county was about 10,000 people with most of them living along highway 29 that goes toward Charlottesville. There was almost no one living in the part of the county where the cabin was located. There were about 200 people living within the Syria zip code. From the cabin to the nearest town, five miles away, there are about 100 people. In the hollow where we live there were about 15 people. The locals who lived there were friendly and taught us how to live and enjoy the tranquility of mountain life. They also taught us about the trees, the animals, the care of the forest and how to live a simpler life as the locals in Claiborne taught us about how they lived off the water. When I was there, my blood pressure was a healthy normal and it was often psychologically painful when we had to pack up after a long weekend to return to Arlington, which was then growing at a fantastic rate. By 2000, after a heart valve replacement it was time to phase out of the law office. We spent more time in the cabin and on rainy days when we needed groceries we would go to Charlottesville. After going in and out of the place many times we got to know the city and slowly found it attractive.

When I met Jennifer and we got involved I had one requirement and that was, we could live anywhere she wanted as long as I could walk to work. The house on Swann Street was a mile from my office and I walked to work every day. In 1985 the office moved to Arlington and a year later we bought a house that was about a mile from the new office and I was back to walking to work. This love for walking to work carried over to Charlottesville where in the 1990's we discovered a lovely downtown section and a number of surrounding neighborhoods and places where a person could walk. I still had a few clients and thought about opening an office in Charlottesville, which was only 40 miles from the cabin. Buying a house in town seemed attractive. I was slowly changing my mind about Charlottesville.

Living in the mountain cabin on a full time basis was fantastic. But there was a major problem. We were young retirees with many years left to live. This means that there is a need to secure any financial resources to allow for them to last through these years. The problem is where to invest this money. As an ex-economist and finance major I knew that keeping money in the bank is dangerous because any serious inflationary period could wipe it out. Leaving it in the stock market was also dangerous since the market is always highly flexible with its ups and downs. The one investment that worked out for us over the years was real estate. We bought Swann Street for $30,000 and sold in a few years for close to $200,000. We bought Claiborne for $35,000 and sold it ten years later for $185,000. We seem to have a knack for good real estate investment. About 1999, and still living in Arlington when Megan, our daughter, was about 17 years old I wanted to throw her out of the house for refusing to respect house rules. Jennifer said I could not do it. Instead Jennifer found two old condos for sale close to the house. The one bedroom condo cost $55,000 and the two bedroom cost $63,000. We bought both of them, put Megan and a friend in the two bedroom condo and rented out the other condo. Between the money we got from the rental, the little rent Megan's girlfriend paid and the money we saved since we no longer needed a social worker to keep the family from killing each other, we broke even. It actually worked out well. Megan was only three blocks away and we never saw her home so much. She came home for food, for long distance telephone calls, to watch TV, to do her laundry. In a couple years she announced she was going to the University of Hawaii for a degree. We all cried as we took her to the airport and then got another young lady from a family trying to raise a difficult child to move into the condo. Years later we sold the condos for a nice profit. The one-bedroom sold for about $170,000 and the two-bedroom sold for over $260,000. To sum up the story, I told everyone that I threw my daughter out of the house. She tells everyone. "Daddy bought me a condo." In the end we made enough money to put our two children through college.

We ended up investing in three houses in Charlottesville, all of them a short walk to the city center and all had nice yards and off street parking. One was an old farm house in an upscale section that we rented out, another was a new house in a development with a homeowners association that we quickly learned to dislike and the other - well the other was a challenge and that perked me up. It was a Federal style house in the wrong side of the railroad tracks in a rough neighborhood that showed signs that it may come back. It was for sale for $225,000 and the ad said it was appraised at $250,000. It was dual zoned for residential and commercial. It appeared to be a perfect place to have a law office. I called the broker and she agreed to meet us at the house and when we got there, Julie was waiting and told us she would not go inside because it was dangerous. Reluctantly I ventured inside and immediately realized there was a serious problem with massive amounts of cat urine. It was not possible to stay inside for more than a few minutes, though amazingly the two ladies who lived in the house and who were there at the time seemed to be going about their day to day

                    STANTON BRAVERMAN

business without any concern about the smell or any health issues it created.

The house was intriguing. About three weeks later we called the broker from the mountain cabin and asked if it was still up for sale, which it was and according to the broker it still smelled horrible. I said, "Julie, lets offer a very low price. I know how to get rid of cat urine and I may end up with a nice investment. Offer them $160,000."

That offer was quickly turned down. Julie advised that the owner had a hissy fit when given the contract and said she had already turned down an offer for that amount. "OK Julie, offer them $185,000. Make it a cash offer and I will take it as it is. Tell them settlement to be in 30 days, and if they do not accept it please do not bother to call me back."

Julie called about an hour later and said that they accepted the contract. We had another house with a lot of problems. Thirty days later we settled and it was now my problem. But cat urine can be cured. It takes time. The house has to be kept warm with no sunlight getting in. It also had to be moist. Once that is in place all that is needed is time for the bacteria to eat at the urine. According to the instruction on getting rid of the smell, it was recommended to try to find out if it was a female or male cat that created the problem. Females urinate on the floor and males urinate on the walls. By going into the house at night with an ultraviolet light it is possible to spot the major places where the animal urinated. Once spotted it is a good idea to spray that spot with warm water. But to me it was a great buy and once the smell was gone I would start thinking about remodeling. It was a nice very old house which we bought $65,000 below appraised value. We only needed a couple of months to correct the problem.

It turned out that a lot of the urine was on the wall-to-wall rugs that were all over the house. My son Jonathan and his friends got the job of pulling out the rugs. It was probably the dirtiest job they ever had and by the end of the day the rugs were in a pile by the curb waiting for the trash service to pick them up. They smelled so fowl that all the neighbors called the city to get them out of the neighborhood as quickly as possible. Within a day they were gone and then a miracle happened. With the rugs gone the house no longer had the smell of urine. It was all in the rugs. About a month later, while talking to one of the neighbors we found out what actually caused the smell. "The two ladies who lived there wanted to buy the house but they could only financially qualify for a loan for $160,000. So, in order to bring the price down they took out the kitty litter for the cats and the cats just went ahead and did what cats are supposed to do."

This house was located in the Belmont section of Charlottesville which is located on the other side of the tracks. There is a railroad line that runs through the town and on the East side of the tracks is the downtown commercial section that is surrounded on three sides by nice fancy homes. Belmont was the section that was to be the place where poor whites and blacks were to live. But this was in 2003 and neighborhoods such as this in many cities in the United States were coming back. There, old houses were bought and remodeled. Throughout the country this trend was accelerating and to me it was only a matter of time before Belmont went through the same process. It had everything going for it and that was location, location and location. It was a nice house that needed a massive amount of remodeling, a great flat back yard with room to park cars and still have a huge veggie garden. Everything was in walking distance. If a person lived there he would seldom need to use his car. A few houses in the area had already sold and were remodeled by recently married hippy types – similar to the way it was when I bought the house on Swann Street. They bought the houses at low prices and with 'sweat equity' fixed them up room by room. The neighbors who were fixing up one of these houses came up to congratulate me on the great deal we got. One neighbor said to me, "How did you get such a steal on that house?" and when I told him about the cat urine he just did not believe how we lucked out in getting such a nice house at a great price.

Jennifer and I knew the neighborhood would come back. We had seen Swann Street change; we had seen Claiborne change and we had seen the community in Arlington change over time. In every case it was exciting to live in a "comeback neighborhood." They are exciting places to live while they are changing. But as they changed and the neighborhoods became desirable places to live, the price of the houses

          STANTON BRAVERMAN

would go up and eventually they would become so expensive that only rich folks could live there. We knew that Belmont would change and then change some more and in the end it would end up being a neighborhood we preferred not to live in. But until then it would be a great place to live. We had been through these changes and seen how it worked. We fully understood the economics behind this trend. It was not taught at the university but rather it is knowledge a person gets through life's experiences,

Let's go back in time once more to 1965, when I was a MBA student at Temple University and working during the day as a high school teacher at one of the worst rated schools in the city located in a difficult poor ghetto area, While at the library working on a term paper about urban renewal I read an interesting study by a professor at the University of Michigan. At that time there were a lot of studies about rebuilding the inner cities. Most of the inner cities had become ghettos where large numbers of people lived at the poverty level. There was urban blight of run-down boarded up old row houses, many stores were closed and there was a high crime rate. The civil rights movement was calling for changes in these neighborhoods. But no one could come up with a decent idea on how to get it to happen. One ridiculous proposal that was seriously being considered called for the leveling of large sections of the inner city and then building houses of the type that were built in the suburbs. While the academic community seems to accept this approach, the civil rights groups were against it. The rally cry against this threatened development was "Urban removal is Negro removal," which was exactly what the issue was all about. The article rationally pointed out that urban renewal could not happen because energy prices were too low. That year gasoline sold for about $.40 a gallon and it was cheaper and easier for a middle class worker to live in the suburbs in a house that was poorly insulated than live in the city closer to work. The poor could not afford the suburbs and they lived in the city. With most of the people with financial resources living outside the city, this left behind a tax base so low that the local governments could not provide the poor with basic needs. To make matters worse, some cities took down a number of houses in the ghetto to build interstate highways that allowed the middle class to work in the city and then scoot back to the suburbs at 5:00 pm. The effect was to reduce the number of livable houses and to divide neighborhoods.

By 1969, the year I started to attend law school at night while working as an Economist for the Treasury Department, I was a member of this middle class that left the city every day for Rockville Maryland – a suburb 15 miles from my job at the Treasury. I would spend over two hours a day fighting traffic that was tense and exhausting. During the last three years at Treasury I was going to law school at night. I would drive my car to the public parking lot at Carter Barron, which was about two miles from the office, take my bike off the rack and bike the rest of the way to work. It was through a rough section of the city and at times some of the local teenagers would threaten to take the bike and occasionally throw a stone at me. But during those three years of going to law school I noticed some significant changes. First, the teenagers stopped threatening me or throwing stones. Second I noticed a few houses were being fixed up. Then in 1972, when I graduated law school, left Treasury to start my own office and was about to separate from my wife I needed a place to live. At that time the United States had its first energy crisis. The price of gasoline went to $1 a gallon and, remembering the words of my old professor, I searched for a house in the inner city to buy and ended up with a house on Swann Street. While it was a small house that was built in the 1800s (It was 15 feet wide and 40 feet deep. It was exactly what I wanted; I hated the long commute from Rockville to downtown DC every day. The bus service was impossible to use and I had to drive in order to get to classes in the evening. The only way I could shake off the frustration of the drive was to bike ride the last two miles to the office. Now, living on Swann Street, the office was a few blocks away. It was totally irrelevant that the neighborhood was considered to be one of the most dangerous places in the city, that there were only a couple of middle class single people living there and the rest were poor African Americans. There were local gangs, there were drug sales, there would be gunshots and police car sirens blasting all night. That did not bother me because I had the ability to walk to work. In those days the mayor was Marion Barry who

STANTON BRAVERMAN

was a controversial civil rights leader with some serious drug issues. He made the newspapers across the nation on a number of occasions and was viewed by the intelligentsia as the paragon of corrupt inner city government. It is true that his administration was corrupt but it was focused on finding jobs for his people and he overstaffed the city departments with huge number of jobs. Barry's political concept was easy to understand and that was "The White Man ripped of the Black man for hundreds of years and now it was time for the Black Man to rip off the While Man". What was interesting is that his plan worked. Poor Blacks found desk jobs with the city even though many of them were not qualified for them. They made a decent salary and they dreamed of being middle class. They bought houses in the suburbs and sent their children to local schools that were highly rated. The payback to society happened with the children, who proved they were good students and went on to college. As a result, today the largest and most secure middle class Black community is in the DC suburbs.

The mayor was excited when a few "pioneers" arrived who were living in the ghettos. That was because he knew we had money and that is what he wanted. It was money to pay the staff and to provide some services to poor families. To do this he had to keep us happy and that was easy to do. The police came through the neighborhood and told all the drug dealers to leave us alone, the city trash department was told to pick up the trash, Swann Street was now clean and best of all, whenever there was a problem in the neighborhood and the police were called they would quickly be there. When I met Jennifer and she moved in, we both loved the city and the neighborhood. But it slowly changed and one by one the houses on the block were sold and remodeled and the poor African Americans moved out and middle class families moved in. I guess we would have stayed on Swann Street for years but soon we had Megan and then we needed a larger house: also my office moved to Arlington and I could no longer walk to work. Besides, the neighborhood had changed. By 1986 most of the redevelopment on Swann Street and the surrounding area was done by gay men. They made fantastic changes to the neighborhood and became great neighbors. I became friends with a number of them and in the morning while walking to work I would meet up with them and we would walk down 15ᵗʰ street together. But as more gays moved into the area it became nationally known as a gay neighborhood. This did not bother me until one day when I was at a bookstore on Connecticut Ave and DuPont Circle, while reading the introduction of a book I was about to buy, a gay man snuck up behind me and goosed my ass. I was about ready to punch him out, told him I was not gay and for him to get lost. He then said, "This is a gay neighborhood. If you are here we assume you are gay. Otherwise, just get out of here!" What I did not realize is the extent that gay men had taken over the neighborhood and that it was known to be that way across the country. Years later at a party in Charlottesville I mentioned to the person I was talking to that we used to live on Swann street. The comment was overheard by a gay man who knew of Swann Street and immediately came over to me to ask if I was gay or had once been gay. The neighborhood had changed, the house was too small for the three of us and I could no longer walk to work. I took the advice I got from the man who pinched my ass -we moved on. It was not that much of a move. We went from inner city Washington to the inner part of Arlington Virginia which is on the other side of the Potomac River. "As the crow flies" it was four miles away.

We lived in Arlington for 17 years. Our two children, Megan and Jonathan, went to local schools. When we moved in the neighborhood was mostly homes of middle level government employees. But over time, as the city developed the cost of real estate increased and by the time we moved out we could no longer afford to buy the house. Its original cost was $175.000 was sold for over $650,000. The sale of this house was the third time we played the real estate game. The house on Swann Street, Claiborne and Arlington led to nice profits. What intrigued me about Belmont was that in many ways it was similar to our life on Swann Street. There was an eclectic group of people. Mostly poorer families, a number of yuppie type artists and musicians, a few professionals who opted to live in this part of town. There were also a number of gays and lesbians. There was a recent zoning change that was to encourage the establishment of community stores where people could easily walk to from their homes in Belmont. It was also in walking distance to the

         STANTON BRAVERMAN

downtown section. It had the potential to be an amazing house. The house was architecturally charming, had location, location and location, it had a nice large backyard that allowed for off street parking and it was inexpensive. We jumped at the chance to buy the house and wanted to be there as the neighborhood developed.

But the house in Belmont was in terrible condition and at first we left the house vacant. The electrical system was old, wires were exposed, and the fuse box was too small. The prior tenants installed additional electrical outlets using lamp wire. There was a lot of lead paint on the walls which was flaking. When you walked across the living room the whole house would bounce up and down, which meant that there were hidden structural problems. The roof was in bad shape, though it did not leak. The chimney stack for the gas furnace was original brick and the mortar was weakened by the moisture from the water that was part of the exhaust. The windows were old single-pane glass which allowed massive amounts of cold air to come into the house. At that time we still were living in the cabin and were not planning to quickly return to the inner city. We did not know what to do with the house.

Should we remodel it, and if so, how much remodeling? There are all sorts of levels to remodeling. Sometimes minimum efforts are done, such as painting and maybe some rewiring or a change in a bathroom fixture and other times it be a heavy duty job where the house is gutted and brought back as almost a new house. We knew it needed a lot of work, but just how much? As time went on and after using it as an office, we got a better feel for the house. This is the pattern we followed with every house we remodeled: slowly get to know the house and the neighborhood, watch for new development, and meet the neighbors. We needed to know the house quite well before making such any decision. What we did not know is that this house in a couple of years would become our second home and we would be engaged in an exhausting adventure fighting the City Council. We did not realize that all the social and political forces that led to urban renewal in a small Southern town would fall on Belmont and that the house we bought was "ground zero" in the chaos of this change.

CHAPTER 6

MOVING TO BELMONT

A MONTH LATER my daughter Megan (The daughter I threw out of the house, who later went off to Hawaii, got a dual degree in French literature and drama) and her husband, Chad moved into town and they needed a place to live. When Chad saw the house he announced he would move in as it was, but given that there were so many hidden dangers I refused to let him do so. Instead we decided to fully remodel the house. After remodeling (after long hours of work at the office) the houses on Swann Street, the Eastern Shore, and in Arlington and then building two houses on our mountain property, it looked like a good opportunity to teach Chad how to remodel. That was the beginning of a two year project that had a lot of ups and downs but in the end the project was completed. Megan and Chad never moved in because the marriage fell apart and the house continued to be my part time law office as I attempted to come out of retirement. About the time the marriage failed Megan gave us Chloe.

At that time the neighborhood was quickly changing. It was at a pace that was a lot faster than expected. We figured it would be about five years before the world discovered Belmont and for a few years at least the neighborhood would be a great place to be. That summer, while working on the remodeling project every weekend, we noticed a number of U-Haul trailers parked on the street as people moved out and others moved in. It was similar to the changes we saw on Swann Street, Arlington and in Claiborne, MD but on an accelerated level. While this transformation of the neighborhood was going on, it justified a change of plans. At first the remodeling project focused on upgrading the electrical and installing a central air conditioning system. The rest, as they say in the trade, would be lipstick. Just things to make it look updated would hide a lot of ugly things. The major issue in remodeling is how far to remodel. It is a lot different than building a house where the plans are made, the building supplies come by truck and the house is built as if it is a kid's elector set. Remodeling is much harder. It can be anything from a patch up and paint project to a serious remodeling effort. Also with remodeling it is hard to determine where to start and when to stop. The old material that is still good has to match up with the new material that the supply houses now sell. Overall, while building a new house is an engineering project, remodeling is more like an art project.

The house the author remodeled in Belmont, Charlottesville.

At that point our decision was to gut the house down to the bone and bring it back. It needed too much stuff and could not be done little by little over a number of years. Often it is better and cheaper to gut than do it piecemeal. Since the neighborhood appeared to be quickly improving the additional cost of a major remodeling was justified.

The first step was to get a demolition permit from the city building inspector's office. The town office building was four blocks away, across the railroad tracks and one block along the downtown mall on Main Street. It was a nice day and a nice walk. The staff in the inspector's office was polite and helpful. They asked a lot of questions about the job and if there was a problem with lead paint being stripped from wood or if there was asbestos in the walls. The house was built 20 years before asbestos was used in plaster and most of the lead paint that had flaked off the woodwork was vacuumed out. The only lead paint that existed was on the molding and that would be pulled off. Soon I was walking back across the bridge to Belmont with the demolition permit. As I crossed I stopped off at Spudnuts for a donut. Spudnuts is an old donut chain from the 1950s that years ago closed down. This was the last of the Spudnuts. It got its name because the donuts were made with potato flour. Once inside the shop a customer immediately went back in time to the 1950's. The staff wore white uniforms from that period; the coffee was only $.50 a cup. In the corner were a number of older locals who met for coffee and donuts and gossip every day. With a spudnut in one hand and a cup of coffee in the other I walked the two blocks back to the house.

The next step was to get a rolloff and a johnny-on-the-spot. A rolloff is a huge dumpster that is delivered by a truck that rolls off the back. It was put in the backyard. The idea is to fill it with all of the debris. Then I needed to find a crew because it was too much of a job for me and Chad to do alone. I walked uphill to the corner to the Belmont Market where a number of locals hung out and asked if anyone was interested in working on the job. None of them were interested in the work. They are an interesting group of poor people who have been hanging out in front of the store for a long time. They have been close friends for many years. The neighborhood will change, the Yuppie class will move in. But these folks will still come back to this one spot for years to catch up on whatever it is that interests them. The rich man has the country club to go to meet people he relates to. The middle class all have a favorite bar or coffee shop to go to. And if you are poor and cannot afford to spend money for booze or coffee then you hang out at a local store. It is their meeting place and it is important to them. Over the years, living on Swann Street and other similar communities I have grown to understand and welcome their presence in the neighborhood. They are a friendly bunch, they will tell you what is going on, they will watch over your property and give you a great "hello, how you doing" greeting that will stay with you for a good part of the day.

While I was going around asking for volunteers, four Mexican workers showed up and announced they would help for $10 an hour plus lunch. They found out about the job from one of the men at the Market. We agreed, I gave them hammers, crow bars, work gloves and face masks and instructions that they had to use the face masks which they seemed not to like.

We soon filled up the rolloff and called to have it hauled away and a bigger one brought over. We soon filled that one and it was hauled away and another came. By the time we had the house gutted we filled four of them. One load alone weighed 13 tons. And the work went on for three weeks. We all worked together hitting the wall with the hammers and cracked the old plaster and then put it into buckets and then into the dumpster. We used the crowbar to pull down the molding along the floors and the windows. Once it seemed like the place was gutted it took two or more days to clean up the mess. It was then I was able to see how the old house was built and how to proceed in remodeling. It became clear that not only did the electrical and plumbing need to be replaced but it turned out that the house, as grand as it looked, was poorly built as if the builder knew the lipstick trick and a lot of the new materials that we wanted to use to bring it back again did not mesh into the old material. For example, the old wall studs were a true 2 x 4 inch stud while the new studs are somewhat less though called 2 x 4". When a bad stud was pulled out we could not just put a new stud in its place. In addition, most of the old studs for the interior walls were twisted and at times crooked. The builders a hundred years ago could do this because the walls were finished with wet plaster and they could easily cover up such defects. Today the builders use sheet rock and it only work if the all the studs are straight.

The studs for the exterior part of the house were straight and in place, except there was one minor problem. The house was built with balloon construction. That is when the studs go straight up for two floors and there is an air space between the floors. Today this type of construction is illegal because it is a serious fire hazard, and whenever possible have to be corrected. The air space, in the event of a fire, will quickly allow the fire to engulf the whole house. Correcting the problem is easy when the walls are gutted and the basic structure is exposed. A piece of a 2 x 4 inch stud cut 16 inches long will fit in the open space and cut off any draft that could feed a fire. The problem was easy to fix with a piece of a stud covering up the space. A hundred years ago balloon construction served a purpose. The air flow in the walls allowed for the house to be cooler on hot days. Gas, wood or coal, which was used to heat the house, was cheap, and they did not have air conditioning. Today, energy is expensive; the current idea is to insulate the house to keep in the cool or hot air and the fire blocks now are required. It is actually cheaper to cool a house with air conditioning than heat the house.

The house was originally had parallel wiring, which is where the wires (the hot and cold wire or the + or − wire ran about two feet from each other across the top of the rafters. Over time some of it was replaced but a lot of it was still hot and if touched could cause an electrical shock. It had to be taken out.

The scariest defect was the way the iron beam went from the front door across the living room to the staircase. It was there to support all of the floor joists on the second floor. It was resting on one old 2x4 that came down the wall to the bottom of the first floor. That was insane and that was the reason why the house seemed to be insecure. At a minimum there should be two 2x4s holding up the beam and they should extend all the way to the basement and rest on solid concrete.

There were only three interior items that were saved. The first was the gas boiler that appeared to be no more than ten years old, the second was the old pine floors and the third was the old radiators for heat. Everything else in the interior was removed. Slowly it was put back together and about a year and a half later it was complete. I then reopened the law office in the house and was back to being a lawyer on a part time basis. We live in the cabin and I would drive into Charlottesville two or three days a week to meet with clients.

But one other problem soon surfaced that messed up our comfortable life living in Madison County, Jennifer, my lovely wife, wanted to be a full time grandmother to Chloe. At first, she set up a couple of rooms on the second floor for us to spend a night here and there when in the city. Then her grandmother duties turned out to be almost a full time arrangement and we were in Charlottesville four or five nights a week. Then one day Jennifer announced that I had to move the office out of the house because it slowly became her place to nest and the office was in her way. Instead we agreed to build a 600 square foot addition on the side of the house with a separate entrance to be the office. It would be two rooms plus a full bath. That was another year of work and an interesting story which I will get to later. By that time the neighborhood started to turn around to be a nice place to live, and it was a lovely house. It had all new walls, windows, electric wiring, plumbing, new kitchen. The old floors were redone, the old radiators provided the most comfortable heat in the winter of any house we ever had and Jennifer just loved being a grandmother to a grandchild who needed her.

The addition was all new material and turned out to be charming. It was a perfect place for a law office.

But then, Eddie Summers, who was the associate in my office, announced that he wanted to go out on his own. Eddie is a nice young fellow and it was not a bad idea that he do so, but I just did not want to work by myself. I was then over 70 years old and it was time to slow down. I told Jennifer that I was not going to reopen the office and she jumped for joy when she realized that not only did she get all of the old house but the whole addition. "I do not believe it. I am living in my perfect dream house in a town with lots of space and in walking distance to everything."

CHAPTER 7

THE FIRST WAR AGAINST THE COUNCIL

AT THIS POINT we once more have to go back in time, but only to about the time we bought the house. Shortly after buying the house and before it was redone, I was walking our dog down the street to meet the neighbors. Belmont is a front porch neighborhood where residents often sit on their porch and talk with everyone who passes by. One of the neighbors I met that night welcomed me to the neighborhood and gave me some information; I did not realize its importance at first. He said, "This is a great town and a great neighborhood with a lot of nice people. But there is one thing you have to remember is that the City Council is your worst enemy." The statement took me by surprise. A person would expect that if the people were nice then the City Council would also be that way. At first I did not give serious attention to the warning. I just thought the neighbor was upset about some minor issue that was before the Council. But it did not take long before I understood what he was talking about. Located across the street from our house and up two doors is the old Dr. Pepper bottling building. It was a quaint old building with huge wooden beams. It was not as huge as most bottling plants are today but still large. It had been a used furniture store for many years on one floor and in the walkout basement was an electrical wiring shop. The Easter family bought it from the Eastern family and Jeff Easter, who is a talented remodeler, redid the place into a number of businesses. There were two restaurants. One called La Taza, which means "cup" in Spanish and was a first class coffee shop. The second was a rather large restaurant called Bel Rio. This restaurant part was sponsored by the old C and O restaurant that had been a favorite in the city for many years. It was a nice plush place to eat that served good food. The owner told everyone in the neighborhood that there would be light music and that they had spent a lot of money for sound mitigation. At first Jennifer and I were excited to see the redevelopment of the plant. They appeared to be an upscale business that would operate in a rapidly changing community.

Soon the restaurant opened and it quickly became apparent that the place would not succeed. Restaurants are strange. There is always a gamble about whether it will be a success. There were already three restaurants on the Belmont Corner that were successful – Mas, the Local and La Taza. But Bel Rio failed. When the owners realized what was happening they suddenly tried to salvage their investment and turned it over to a new operator. He turned it into a loud music venue that stayed open until 2:00 am. It then attracted the late night crowd that borders on being drug addicts and the noise was far above the safety level. There were cheap bands that played loud music that could be heard through the whole neighborhood. This seriously disrupted the lives of anyone who lives in near the Corner. Many elderly folks were unable to get to sleep until the music stopped. In addition, customers could be seen at night sneaking back to their cars for a taste of liquor which was a cheap way to get drunk or they would sneak into someone's yard and urinate. The quality of the people who were the late night customers was about the lowest level of human being that could be found anywhere. The noise ordinance seemed to allow the loud music and it was necessary to get the City Council to change the noise regulations. But the new owner, Jim Baldi, was known as a local businessman and accountant and the City Council gave him strong support. The entire neighborhood complained and the local newspaper covered the story. The Council discussed it at a meeting. The Mayor claimed that the business was providing jobs for local musicians and they just did not want to move on the issue.

The problem went on for about a year and the Council constantly refused to effectively deal with Mr Baldi. The Council again said that the restaurant was providing jobs for local musicians. But soon Baldi changed the nature of the business and hired a DJ (disc jockey) who played amplified music from CDs. The bands were gone. For some unexplainable reason this brought in a larger crowd from Richmond and other nearby cities. The noise got louder and the City Council still refused to act, still claiming that Baldi was a leading and responsible businessman. Yet, every Saturday night the police cars were there to keep order and to issue tickets for the massive number of customers who were urinating in the neighbors' front yards. At times the neighbors would meet with Bel Rio's landlord, Jeff Easter, and ask why he did not evict the owner and Jeff would say there was nothing he could do. At times we would meet with an investigator with the Alcohol Beverage Control Board who was willing to work with us in getting the license withdrawn. But we soon realized that Baldi was not concerned about keeping his license because he had not paid the fee to renew his corporate charter which meant that technically he was out of business and his license was not valid. This information was given to the inspector and they did shut the place down for three nights until he paid and renewed the charter. The noise continued and then we would once again ask Jeff if he could do something and it was then that Jeff told me that the lease only allowed for Baldi to play quiet music because he know loud music would disrupt the neighborhood.

The neighborhood continued to go back to the City Council and eventually the Council agreed to reduce the noise level from 80 decibels to 60 decibels. Jim Baldi always got the right to speak first and his major statement was that Belmont was a very bad neighborhood until he opened Bel Rio and it improved things. A couple members of the City Council would thank him for his efforts. Then a few musicians who worked at the restaurant at times would thank the Council for allowing them to screw over the neighborhood.

Eventually the Council started to change its views and agreed to lower the legal noise limit. But then it was a question on where to read the decibel meter. The Council said that the reading should be at the local residences and not at the place of business. That basically left the level as it was because a strong base could carry quite far and at 60 decibels was enough to make the windows rattle. The neighborhood

 STANTON BRAVERMAN

was powerless against the Council. And the warning I got from about the Council being my worst enemy became true. It was clear that the Council did not care about Belmont. To them it was a place to gather a number of poor people of all races and the welfare of these folks was to be ignored. We soon learned that the Council was only interested in meeting the needs of The University of Virginia and the hospital and those sections of the town and the county where the upper class lived. To them Belmont was a place where the poor live and in that section of town the city would allow anything to happen.

Jennifer and I were able to escape this horror on weekends when the noise was the loudest because we would return to the cabin. But every time I left the area I felt sorry for the neighbors who stayed behind and who would be up half the night. I started to review the law trying to find some way to undercut the City Council.

One thought was to bring a legal action based on the lease Jeff said he had with Baldi. If the lease said that there was to be quiet music which was for the benefit of the neighborhood then we could claim we are a third party beneficiary to the lease and therefore have the right to file an action in court. There was also research about the possibility of getting the place closed down as a public nuisance. That encouraged us to make videos of the customers going to their cars to get a sip of booze or of them walking outside when urinating with an alcoholic drink in their hand. This should be enough to get the ABC to revoke the license and, even if Baldi ignored it, the ABC would shut him down. In order to make this argument in court we would need a copy of the lease and it was not clear if Jeff would give it to us. But a copy of the lease should be with the ABC in order to get a liquor license and the ABC inspector said he could provide it to us.

The continued fight with the Council and the chaos that came to the neighborhood from Bel Rio brought together all the neighbors; I did not know many of them at the time. That is when we met Alyson Flavia Ruffner, who told us she was an ex jockey, opera singer and internet technician and actress, which all turned out to be true. Alyson is a scrappy person and is a female version of John Wayne in that she is rough and tough and does not take shit off of anyone. She would be at Bel Rio with a decibel reader late at night and taking notes of what it read. She would call the police when it was too high which was on a daily basis. But the police never did anything. It seemed that just before they arrived the noise would be turned down which suggested that someone in the police department would be warning them, or when the police arrived they forgot to get the official sound meter to measure the noise, or if they had the meter they were not sure where to take the reading. It seemed as if the city government just did not care about Belmont.

Janet Hatcher owned the building across the street from Bel Rio. It was a corner building that was a combination store and living quarters that was built probably more than a hundred years ago. At one time her deceased husband used the store as a photography studio. But now the store part of the building was boarded up. Janet would often sit on her side porch feeding whole peanuts to squirrels that lived in the huge ash trees on her property, which shaded most of the Belmont Corner. Many times while walking Kodie I would come by and she would complain about the noise, the chaos at night and how Baldi was destroying a nice neighborhood. Janet should have the official title of Belmont Historian because she lived there for most of her life and worked at times with her father in the Belmont Market, which was across the street from her house. She was often upset with the way things were going, especially when the City Council and other city officials would be telling the public that Bel Rio and Jim Baldi saved Belmont. She would be the first one to point out that Baldi was insulting the neighborhood and would get upset when the City Council supported Baldi's statements. To her it was bad enough when Baldi put down the neighborhood, but when the Council agreed with him it became an insult to the city and to everyone who lived here. She would point out that they knew better and that the Mayor actually was born and raised in Belmont. To her, Belmont was a great and exciting place to live. While it was not the rich section of the city and many of the local residents were poor, there was camaraderie among the locals that tied them together. The city basically had almost nothing to do with that section of town and spent most of its revenue on the upper class places and section surrounding the University. They

STANTON BRAVERMAN

knew nothing about the lives of the people living there. I guess in a sarcastic way it can be said they were right in saying that Bel Rio saved Belmont because for the first time in many years the City Council took notice of that section of town.

Actually that is not quite true. A few years before Bel Rio opened the City Council at the recommendation of the office for neighborhood planning rezoned the area around Downtown Belmont to be called The Belmont Business Corridor. At the time there were no real businesses. But the hope was to allow for a few shops to open that would serve the local neighborhood. Since the shops were for the locals and it was walking distance for anyone living in Belmont it was not necessary to include parking lots or parking facilities. In poor neighbors the ratio of the number of cars to the population is very low. There would be 6 or more people living in one house and maybe there would be one car, while in the upscale sections there would be 2 or 3 people living in a house and there would be at least two cars. But Bel Rio did not fit into this plan. Almost all of the customers were from the surrounding counties; there would be as many as 150 of them in the place on a weekend, There were no parking lots for the cars and at night it was impossible for the local residents to find a place to park their own cars.

Down the street a short way you can find the Mas Restaurant where Tomas is the chef. It is a tapas place with a European style patio by the sidewalk where the food is fantastic. Jennifer and I would at times sit there and have a couple of tapas with a great glass of wine and fantastic cheeses. This one cluster of buildings – Mas, Janet's place, Bel Rio and the remodeled soda plant, and three other restaurants was unofficially known as Downtown Belmont. It is in a very old section of the town with narrow streets that all seem to come together. Meridian, Carlton, Hinton, Douglas and Monticello Drive all come together at one corner. Because there are a number of families at the poverty level in Belmont many of the men ride small motor scooters and I remember on night sitting at Mas' patio having a glass of wine with Julie Gee, the real estate broker who sold us three houses in Charlottesville, and commenting that between the neighbors walking their dogs, whizzing by of motor scooters and the clinking of the dishes and glasses at Mas it was similar to a back street in Paris. The neighborhood was charming and the restaurant customers were from the surrounding suburbs who enjoyed the local character. They would park their high-priced luxury cars in front of our house and we could hear them from the bedroom room window as they laughed about the delightful evenings they had. In this environment Bel Rio just did not belong. His customers did not show up until 12 pm and peed all over the town and yet the City Council held up Baldi as an upstanding leading citizen for saving Belmont.

I remember going to Council meetings when they discussed the noise issue. I would sign up. As usual, the first person to speak was Jim Baldi who would get everyone upset by once again telling the Council that Belmont was known as a dumpy area and his business actually was an improvement. When I got the chance to speak, which was limited to three minutes, I would tell the Council that Belmont was a comeback neighborhood and it was in their best interest to make it a decent place to live. I told them that I lived on Swann Street in Washington DC when it was a comeback place. At that time Marion Barry was the mayor and he ran a better city government than they did because he knew that with the improvement in the neighborhood, real estate taxes and other sources of revenue the city needed would increase. But the members of the Council did not realize that there was a national trend toward urban renewal and just ignored what I told them. They looked at me as if I was crazy and they just could not accept the fact that maybe there was something of value in Belmont. Or maybe they just could not accept the fact that Marion Barry ran a better city government than they did because, as I said before and I will repeat, it is a very haughty town. When townspeople are haughty they will only focus on what they see of value as they define it and will pay no attention to the rest of the community. Haughty people see the world through narrow eyes. They feel that their way of life is the only way to live and will never admit that they are wrong. At any price, at any time and in any way they will never concede that they made a mistake. When confronted with a true fact that they are wrong they will find a way to drop the subject and slowly slink away. Then once the conversation is over they will act as if

　　　　STANTON BRAVERMAN

it never happened. In the end they do not learn from their mistakes as normal people do.

While the neighborhood was fighting with the Council over Bel Rio, Bob Fenwick appeared at our doorstep to ask if there was anything he could do to help us. Bob is a local contractor and at the time aspired to run for a seat on the Council and had tried to do so as an independent candidate. Bob is a quiet man, who thinks before he talks and measures his words. He has lived in the city for years, his wife is an attorney and they have a nice home in a very old historical building in the middle of the historical section. Bob took pictures of the chaos at the restaurant and took sound readings with a sound meter. But he could not get the Council to do something about the noise level that was destroying the neighborhood. There were a number of articles in the local newspapers about the noise issue with people writing in all sorts of obnoxious comments such as "Put ear plugs in your ears and that will deal with the noise." Or, "Everyone knows that Belmont is a dangerous place in town and Jim had done a lot to clean it up."

In the middle of this controversy the Belmont Carlton Neighborhood Association was formed with the assistance of the city government and Jim Baldi, The person who was chosen to be the head of the organization was a young musician who supported the noise level that Baldi thought was appropriate. It was strange going to City Council meetings where there would be a number of local residents to complain about the noise while the Council would only pay attention to the representative from the so-called neighborhood association and they based their decision on the recommendations of the association.

There are other important characters that have to be mentioned in order for the reader to get a clear picture of downtown Belmont. There is Shirley Shotwell who lives next door to us. She is a country woman who grew up on a farm about 20 miles outside of town. She lives in a cottage style house with her niece, Hope and her handicapped brother, Kenny. Shirley is retired and spends a lot of time on her porch greeting everyone that comes by. She got the worst of the Bel Rio noise because she is directly across the street from Bel Rio and she spent many sleepless nights trying to duck the loud noise. She is a quiet person, simply dressed, the type that is often referred to as "the salt of the earth" Over the years we have gotten close to her and her family which means we often have to drive her to a doctor's appointment. Jennifer and I have been on her porch so many times that Kodie, our 90 pound lab/husky will often, without us knowing it, go over to her house and stay for a few hours. It is his second home and Hope now insists that Kodie is her dog.

It looked like the only way to end this problem with Bel Rio was to file an action in court. While I was getting close to filing it, strange things started to happen. We kept hearing rumors that the FBI was investigating Jim Baldi and that sooner or later he would be in serious trouble. We did not know if there was any truth to the rumor, or if true, what the investigation was all about. The rumors did not make sense because the City Council kept praising the man and if there was such an investigation the City Council probably would have known about it and backed off from praising him.

Then one day Baldi put up a sign that Bel Rio would be closed while he was on vacation. But actually he and his young girlfriend were not going on vacation. They were skipping town. He grabbed as much money as he could from the business and from the local restaurants where he handled the payroll and deposits. Credit card payments ended up in his account, tax filings were never done and the money disappeared. The City Council had to eat mud the next day. As I understand it, Baldi took off right before the FBI was about to arrest him. At the next City Council meeting an embarrassed Council unanimously rewrote the noise ordinance to stop loud noise venues when located near residential homes. But, as already stated. haughty people are not able to learn from their mistakes because they refuse to ever admit they did something wrong. When faced with the fact that they made a mistake they will blink and then go on as if nothing ever happened which only meant that they will venture on to something equally or more irresponsible.

While Jim Baldi did a lot to denigrate the neighborhood there were a number of other local characters that were in their own special way, rather charming and were an important part of the community.

 STANTON BRAVERMAN

At the far end of the bottling plant and across the street is an old gas station that no longer sells gas but Jeff Fitzgerald, who owns the place, sells tires. He has a collection of tires of odd sizes that at times he sells to one of the poorer locals whose old car needs a tire that does not have enough tread on it to pass inspection. It is also the place where we get new tires for the cars, as do a lot of the other neighbors. Jeff is a big man and can throw a tire around like a kid can throw a baseball. He has fixed flats in minutes and can jack up a car faster that I can get out of it. He is a great asset to the community. There have been times when the check tire pressure light would go on in my car. I will drive it the 100 yards to his station and ask for him to check it out. I will then walk home and drink a cup of coffee and then walk back. The car will be waiting. Whatever was the problem, Jeff got it right again. If you ever tour the neighborhood you will quickly see Jeff's garage. On the side of the station that faces Monticello Drive there is an artistic sign attached to his wall that says "I love Charlottesville a lot". It has turned out the be an interesting piece of art and every May, when graduation day is getting close, you will find many graduating students under the sign taking a souvenir picture. At times when I was walking to the local health club I would stop and look at the group and offer my services to photograph all of them in one picture. They would always take up the offer and I would take a picture of a group of excited students under the artwork holding hands, hugging and all them with great smiles. It is clear that they love Charlottesville. But obviously they did not live in the Belmont section.

Across from Jeff's tire station there is the Belmont BQ. It is mostly a takeout restaurant that is owned by the brother of Melissa Easter who owns La Taza. Customers have told me that the BBQ is good but that is one food I am allergic to so I cannot confirm that fact. But Kodie will clearly support that statement. Whenever we walk past the front door he will bark for a morsel of food. He usually gets a least a bite and sometimes it is more than enough for his evening meal. Melissa Easter and her husband Matt can often be found somewhere in the coffee shop or the outside Tiki Bar which is frequented by many of the locals on hot nights. I probably left out mentioning at least a half dozen other important characters that make up Downtown Belmont. If the reader is interested, I recommend they come here and see the place for themselves.

CHAPTER 8

THE SECOND WAR WITH THE COUNCIL

THERE WAS ONE other issue that was adding to the chaos. Next to the BBQ is a charming old southern style house that was zoned as residential. While the Bel Rio fiasco was going on a local businessman bought the old building and said he lived there with his wife, though no one ever saw him there. One day he submitted an application to the zoning board to change the zoning to allow for him to use it as a restaurant that would serve Cajun style foods. It was to be called "The Southern Crescent" but the locals quickly referred to it as the Gumbo Palace. Everyone was concerned about having one more restaurant come into the corner since it already had a number of them and there was almost nowhere to park additional cars. There was a meeting of the neighborhood community organization and the developer told us he was concerned about the noise and would leave all the nice shrubbery in place as noise mitigation; he made other promises such as he would not increase the size of the building when the zoning was done. We knew that he was not telling the truth because what he told us was on the verge of being idiotic. He stated that after buying the house and living in it he realized that there was an awful smell of BBQ coming into the house. He wanted to sell the house but he found out that the BBQ smell significantly affected the value of the house and the only thing he could do to get his money back was to turn it into a restaurant. The only people that believed that story were sitting on the City Council. We still did not agree with the idea of the rezoning and I guess we just did not trust him and at the City Council meeting most of the neighbors objected to the rezoning. But again, the City Council just did not care what the people of Belmont wanted. Again it was the poorer end of town and they had no voice in the decision. The Council approved the rezoning, once again verifying that they are our worst enemy. Two days before that change the developer took out the shrubs and enlarged the patio to include almost the entire side yard (so much for his promise not to enlarge the size of the building.) When I asked them who told them they could do this they told me that Brian Haluska, who worked for the Neighborhood Planning office (NPO,) told them they could do it providing it was done before the day of the official rezoning date. We were upset and angry because what they did was the exact opposite of what they told us they were going to do. They had told us one thing and told the city another thing. Our mistake was meeting with them without a representative of the NPO being there. It was a nice little trick that they pulled on us but we learned that there would be no more meetings with developers without a representative from NPO being there. I emailed Brian and asked why he told the developer to do what he did. Brian emailed me back to say that it was his professional responsibility to so advise the developer and that if he failed to do it he could be in breach of his ethical responsibility as a member of the American Neighborhood Planners Association. I went to the NPA web site and noticed that there was a procedure for bringing an ethical complaint; then I emailed Brian that I was considering filing such a complaint, which then led to a three page memo from his boss, Jim Tolbert, telling me the filing of an ethics complaint was not justified. In the end I did not file the complaint and felt that maybe Brian got the message to stop playing around with the neighborhood. Finally, it should be noted that it has been six years since the zoning change; the building has been gutted, some work was done and then it stopped. It still has not opened. I do not know why it has not opened. It could be a lack of funds, or an illness in the family or the developer just cannot get his act together. Sometime during the year I will meet him on the street and he will greet me as we are the best of friends and once again he'll assure me that he will be opening in a few months. If and when he does he will add more chaos to the neighborhood. Parking issues will get more serious, the local neighbors will complain and they will petition the city to have zoned parking limited to only residents.

 STANTON BRAVERMAN

CHAPTER 9

WHY IS THIS WAR GOING ON?

IN THE END, Baldi left town, the humiliated City Council straightened out the noise ordinance and Bob and I became friends. At that point I felt that, things in Belmont would be getting better and the neighborhood would quickly be improving. My family decided about this time to build an addition for the new office. And since Bob was a contractor, we hired him to be the general contractor. Bob took quite a while to finish the project because he kept taking time off to campaign for a seat as an independent for city council. While he worked on the project we would talk about local political issues and how the city was organized. From the information I got from Bob and others folks that lived in the city I realized that the political structure revolved around a number of very rich people who lived on nice estates that surrounded the town and they had enough money to buy enough voters to get who they wanted on the Council. It also became clear that the control of the city was not with the local residents but with these rich families and all they wanted from the city was a place to put the university and the hospital and to encourage the city to be a holding pen for poor whites and poor blacks. They did it in part by paying the city about $14 million a year under a revenue sharing plane to assure that the city would not expand its borders even though the Constitution for Virginia clearly states that the City cannot expand any further into the county. To me, at the time it did not make sense.

One day while working on the addition I asked why racial relations appeared to be bad within the city.. I have been around African Americans all my life. I went to Overbrook High School right after

Wilt Chamberlain was there. The class was fifty percent Jewish and the other half was poor African American. This was in 1959 about the time the Supreme Court decided Brown v. School Board that required that public schools be integrated. I taught high school at Gratz in Philly which was one of the toughest schools in the city. I lived on Swann Street as the only White man on the block. I guess the reason why I jumped at the chance to buy a house and live on Swann Street is that I developed over the years an understanding and appreciation of the Black culture. It was not intimidating but rather challenging. Their love of the community, the hardship poverty does to them and how they deal with it was something I understood and in a way, living there meant that there was a way for me to help them.

Shortly after moving into Charlottesville I realized that racial relations were not right. It seemed to me that the Black community was extremely angry and beaten down, much more so than I have seen before. It was what you would expect of a Black community at the height of the Jim Crow era. When I lived on Swann Street and I was walking past a Black man, no matter how old or young, no matter how he was dressed, I would always say "How is it going" and he would say the same back to me. At times he would stop me and ask for a match to light a cigarette. Other times he would ask for a dollar. They were very poor people and I understood how poor they were and I often would give a dollar to them. They thanked me and we would go our ways. They needed the money. I knew that and I had it to give and it did not hurt to do so. But in Charlottesville it was different. When you passed a Black man and said "How is it going" He did not respond. He did not even flinch. He would walk by as if I was not there.

I asked around as to the cause of such poor relations and one day Bob told me why it was that way. It all stems from Vinegar Hill. It was their community, with a cluster of old, run-down buildings and stores and business they operated. One year the City decided to take the buildings down and build for that community a modern public housing complex. The Black community did not want to leave and were forced to do so. They liked the way they lived and all they wanted was for the city to fix up a few places. But in taking down the buildings and closing

          STANTON BRAVERMAN

down a lot of their business that never reopened, the City ensured that they gave up hope.

The story shows that the City Council, with its haughtiness and concept that it has infinite wisdom followed the half-assed urban renewal concepts of the 1960's and they proved once again that the rallying cry against it was correct. "Urban renewal is Negro removal" and in Charlottesville it still seems to exist. As a result the local Black community has almost no middle class neighborhood and is still struggling to find a place in our lives. I found out that the City Council is not only my worst enemy but their worst enemy as well.

SEVENTY YEAR OLD IMMIGRATION LAWYER V. THE CITY, THE COUNTY AND THE WATER AUTHORITY.

CHAPTER 10

HOW I GOT INTO THIS MESS

ONE OF THE campaign issues Bob was trying to work on was the restructuring of a three reservoirs that were used by the local water authority that served the county, the city and the university. The plan required the closure of one reservoir that had silted up and to enlarge the dam at Ragged Mountain by raising it by 43 feet. The reservoir at Ragged Mountain could not be filled from the water flowing to it it would be necessary that the water at the reservoir that silted up be pumped nine miles up hill to Ragged Mountain. Bob, who is a civil engineer argued that the old dam should be dredged and that the dam at Ragged Mountain did not need to be enlarged. Bob talked about this a lot as he worked on the house addition and felt that it was a bad investment for the city. He said it was far too expensive for the area to afford and that the current system was good for many more years. There was not a shortage of water; the existing facilities could have gone on for years without making any serious investment. To Bob, a lot of the cost of the dredging of the old reservoir could be paid for by selling the soil that was dredged for top soil that was worth between $300 to $400 a truck load. The soil had been washed down from the Shenandoah National Park, It was fantastic, very rich, without insecticides or chemicals.

While I listened to what he had to say, and he said it to me many times, it was not getting me as upset as it was him. Dams and reservoirs are an important asset to the community and if the enlargement of Ragged Mountain was not the best choice then it could not be as bad as Bob said it was. And also it was the age-old problem with government in that they often do stupid projects based on unjustified public opinion. And besides, while I owned property in the city, officially at that time I was a resident of Madison County and the house on Douglas Street was an investment. If the city and the county wanted to spend money on a dam they did not need, then it was not much of a concern to me.

But that changed one day, right after the addition to the house was completed when Bob asked for me to attend a Council meeting where they are going to vote on the project. I agreed to go and there I was, sitting in the back of the room attending another Council meeting. Because of the Bel Rio fiasco I saw the Council as a group of political hacks that were placating a few politicians who seemed to have control over the city. The distaste I had from the Bel Rio noise issue was still there. The Council public meeting room was full. A lot of people were there to speak against that project. They were not the poor people from Belmont but clearly were educated and professionals. One by one they spoke against the project. One person pointed out that the population growth estimates that supported the claim for the new dam were wrong. Another person stated that dams were not to be built until the State government required that there be a new one and the State had not imposed such a requirement, Another person told the Council that she often walked the trails around Ragged Mountain and loved the old forest and the trees that would be cut down. And why was it necessary to get Nestle Foundation to contribute $500,000 to save the Moorman river that was source of the water that went to the old reservoir? Almost everyone in a packed meeting room was against the dam, with only a couple of people who spoke in favor of the project, and they did not live in the city. It was clear that a significant number of people in Charlottesville and the surrounding county were against the dam. I felt that the Council, with that amount of opposition to the project had to be crazy to approve it. There was an amazing and massive outpouring of arguments against the project. After almost everyone had a chance to speak, the mayor announced rather belligerently, "We heard enough, now let's vote." And then they voted three to two for the project and everyone was pissed off. The real kick in the pants to the local population came from two of the supporting council members who attempted to justify their vote. Councilwoman Kristin Szakos made a strange statement which appeared to me to be about apples and oranges and how it is important that they get together to be fruit salad and Kathy Galvin, who was just elected to the Council on a "Green" campaign, and had just voted to unnecessarily destroy a huge old forest, claimed that future development in the area would be in the county and the county wanted the project and it was necessary for the city to go along with the project to keep the county content. To me the argument was strange and I smelled rats all over the place. The city owned the water rights, the city owned the reservoirs; the county needed the city more that the city needed the county. But based on this childish reasoning they gave away these city assets. In addition Councilwoman Kathy Galvin was wrong to say that the future development in the area would be in the county. She claimed to be skilled in urban development and yet had no idea that urban areas in most cities were coming back and were very much alive. She said the dam would create jobs but did not explain how job creation and the dam were related. As I sat there and saw the Council action at its worst, I realized that the political powers in the city had no interest in meeting the needs of the people. It seemed as if they lived in their own world or there were very strong crony capitalist forces behind what they were doing.

STANTON BRAVERMAN

CHAPTER 11

WHAT IS GOING ON?

J ENNIFER HAS OFTEN said I have a sixth sense about what is happening. She is amazed when I quickly identify a person as not being truthful. I have often walked away from places and groups based on a hunch that things are not right. Almost every time this sixth sense has proven to be correct. At one point in my career as a lawyer I was a partner in a large law firm. Once there I quickly realized that about half the other lawyers in the firm were incompetent and I had to get out of there as fast as possible. One attorney who was a political appointee during the Carter administration looked intelligent, but after you met with him a couple of times it was clear that he was not the type of attorney I wanted as a partner. I felt he was a disaster that could happen at any time. The day the one year commitment to the firm was over I packed up and left as fast as I could even though a number of friends who were attorneys were advising me to stay with the firm. Also, all the other attorneys in the office thought I was too quick to come to a conclusion about the quality of the work coming out of the office and in a way ridiculed me. The senior partners tried to argue with me about leaving. But I was gone. Then about eight months later that one partner, who I thought was an idiot, took on a case that he could not handle which led to a lawsuit for $50 million against the firm and the partners. Since I was gone by then I was not involved in the action. I read someplace that people who are dyslexic may not be good at spelling and get numbers mixed up, but they make up for this handicap by being able to quickly analyze people and difficult situations. And since I am dyslexic (which means I am constantly dialing the wrong telephone number and an idiot at spelling,) this is where the skill came from.

The first stage of the project was $31 million. The pipeline from the old reservoir to the enlarged dam which would cost between $65 million to $100 million would be the second part of the project and that would not be done until there was a serious need to increase the water reserves in the dams. For a small city of 45,000 people and a surrounding county with a population at the time of 90,000 that was an incredible amount of money to spend on a project that was not needed and could have been done a lot cheaper. To me, a paranoid dyslexic attorney, this smelled. After the meeting, I sat there just stunned by the way the meeting went and soon I approached one of the council members who voted against the project and asked "Did the City Attorney sign off on this deal?" The reply was, "The City Attorney said that he did not know if it was legal or not. It did not matter because nobody will file an action in court to stop it and that makes it legal." This only amplified my paranoia that the project was small town corruption at its worst. It is crony capitalism at its worst. It was clear to me that they voted for the project because somebody was going to gain from it and they did not care what the people of the city or the county felt since no one was going to sue them in court to stop their stupidity.

In addition, there was one word that kept coming into my head which reassured me that there was a lot of bad stuff in the project. And that word was "Nestle". I had already read a number of news articles about towns where Nestle had tried to take over water systems. They failed at most of them and it was not clear what Nestlé's interests were with Charlottesville. The company is one of the world's largest bottlers of bottled water and there were reports that they were getting fresh water for their bottling operations without current authorization. To me, their efforts appear devious and suspicious and scary. And this whole project started when the Nestle Foundation gave a grant of $500,000 to a save a river that did not need to be saved.

Nestle sells water under the label of Deer Park and Pollard Springs. I have often seen their trucks delivering massive amounts of drinking water to thousands of business and offices in the Washington DC metropolitan area. To me they appear to be a powerful organization that has to be taken seriously. I began to realize this power when I saw

     STANTON BRAVERMAN

a picture of Obama coming out of a meeting with a bottle of water in his hand. It was Deer Park water and the label was clearly facing the camera for the world to take note of. Then a while later I saw another picture of Obama with a different water bottle that said Pollard Springs and again the label was clearly facing the camera. To operate this business the company needs high quality fresh water and the presence of such water outside of Charlottesville had to be enticing to them. My thinking was somehow or someway were attracted to the reservoir at Sugar Hollow which is where the Moorman river comes out of the National Park.. There was no real reason to save the Moorman River and I felt that maybe they were working on some plan along with Trout Unlimited and Nations Conservancy, both of whom were partners in calling for the project.

The next day, while Bob was cleaning up some of the supplies he used to work on the addition we got into a discussion about the dam. He was upset because Charlottesville was his hometown and he just wanted to see the place work a lot better. We went over everything a second time. Bob again mentioned that the new dam started when the Nestle Foundation and the Nations Conservancy showed up in town with a pledge of a lot of money to "save the Moorman River which started in the Shenandoah National Park and made its way toward Charlottesville," He repeated the fact that along the edge of the mountain chain was a reservoir called Sugar Hollow and it has been said to have the finest water quality in the United States. The plan that the two non-profit organizations had developed was for the dam to hold back a lot of the water and release it so that the river ran all year long. Also Trout Unlimited had shown interest in the project because with water in the river all year long it would enable the local area to use the river for trout fishing. This so-called effort to "save the river" was a fraud for the simple reason that, as everyone in the mountain area knows, during the summer months all the local rivers will dry up. The area is surrounded by dense forest and there are huge trees that absorb a huge amount of water and release it through their leaves at the rate of about 100 gallons a day per tree. This was the natural environment and the idea of keeping a flow of water going all year long was not saving the river. It was a way to create a trout fishing place for wealthy trout fishermen. The land along the river is magnificent and is owned by a lot of very rich people.

At the City Council meeting when they voted on the dam most of the people who spoke against the project did not understand the nuances between the efforts to save the river and the fact that it did not need to be saved. It was clear that this aspect of the project just was not picked up by urban and suburbanites who know very little about the trees and wilderness that surrounds them. I remember at one point I spoke to the attorney for the water authority about this aspect of the project and his comment was. "Do you have a problem saving fish?" I pointed out that the native trout in the river did not need to be saved and that the only fish to be saved would be the rainbow trout that they would later stock in the river once the reservoir at Sugar Hollow was authorized to release water all summer to assure that there would be sufficient water for the Rainbows. I knew from the years I have lived in Madison County in a house that is along the Robinson River, the fact that the rivers dry up. I have seen the Robinson dry up many times and yet the brook trout on the stream seemed to be in good shape. They would find pools of water here and there to hide in until the rains came and the river started to flow again. And this knowledge only added to my concern that the justification for the project by the City Council was not valid.

Recently I found out that exclusive trout fishing spots are now attractive to a number of rich people. It was during a bike ride I took around the village of Syria VA which is where our cabin is located. After riding for about 18 fantastic miles along the Rose River and the Robinson River I stopped at the General Store and bought a candy bar. While eating the chocolate bar on a hot day and seeing it melt all over my fingers I wandered across the street to the community nursery. Steve, the owner of the nursery, was sitting in a chair by one of the hothouses and we talked about what was going on the area. The conversation focused on about a one mile stretch of the Rose River that ran through what had been an old apple orchard. A few years ago it was sold off to be upscale estates for rich people. For years, as I rode the bike down the

          STANTON BRAVERMAN

road past the farm I would see a number of parked cars and pickups. They belonged to the local fishermen who were in the river fishing for the rainbows that the state stocked that week. But when the orchard was broken up and a "no trespassing or fishing sign" was put up, the cars and trucks no longer parked on this part of the river. This was strange, because when a river is stocked with trout by the state then everyone with a fishing license is allowed to enter the property to fish. However, the new owner somehow stopped the public from reaching that part of the river that ran through his property and reserved the right to fish there to whomever he wanted to fish there. Steve told me that a number of rich folks have come down to the area to fish the river and they paid about $185 a day for the right to do so. It was a catch and release program. Trout fishing is now replacing the golf course for the very rich. They can go to exclusive spots where they are well protected from the public and get into the stream with their very expensive gear and throw their fly rod here and there without interference from anyone. It is their way of finding solitude and they have the money to do it. Up the river or even down the river there are still pickup trucks parked along the side of the road where many people who have fishing licenses will fish for trout. At these spots the river is stocked by the state. I do not know how the private fishing reserve is stocked but they may stock it themselves or just rely on the trout that were stocked up the river. But it is clearly big business and that explained to me why there was so much concern in Charlottesville to get the Moorman River to flow all year through the farms that were owned by a number of very rich people.

CHAPTER 12

AND THE FIGHT BEGINS

THERE I WAS at the City Council room, a relatively new resident to the city, seeing them vote on a project that just smelled bad. The pieces just did not tie together. Nestle Foundation grant, a huge number of people upset with the project, the serious issue as to whether or not the city needed the project. "Bob, I think I will sue then to get the project declared illegal". Bob replied, "Stan, are you going to take on the biggest law firm in Virginia?

"Bob, these law firms are a joke and in my immigration practice I took on law firms that were a lot bigger than these firms and against some very qualified lawyers. Bob, I have sued the US government and their law firm is known as the Department of Justice. That is a real law firm and they do not mess around. McGuire Woods is a small time operation compared to the DOJ and probably incompetent. They do not scare me". Then I told him I would figure out an argument to get me into court and then once there all chaos will develop and maybe we can get to the bottom of this issue. Bob pushed me on to do it.

I started researching the issues. At that time I did not know anything about the law and organization of water authorities. But the computer allowed for me to rapidly learn it. I was not up to date on the Code of Civil Procedure for Virginia since most of my law practice involved federal agencies and federal courts. I knew nothing about water rights, and I needed to prepare the case for a possible appeal to the Virginia Supreme Court. To learn all of this I spent hours on the internet reading cases, law review articles and regulations and the state code. Some of the information I needed could not be found on the internet, so I had to spend a number of hours in the law library at the University of Virginia. In a couple of weeks I had drafted a petition for an injunction to stop the project on the grounds that they violated due process of law standards. While it was a valid argument it was rather complicated and Judges hate complicated legal reasoning. They like it to be simple. But it would at least get me into court. Bob announced to the press that I was filing the action and the papers then tried to interview me but I was not interested in publicity. But Bob dragged me out for a press conference.

The major argument related to the issue of the sale of part of the reservoir to the county. The Constitution for Virginia said that the sale of any real estate owned by the City government could only be done by a vote of a super majority of the Council. That meant it had to be a four out of five vote and not a three out of five vote. The City kept saying that there was no transfer of title to the county for any property. Yet, the agreement between the city and the county over the project could be seen as a deed of sale. It met all the statutory requirements for a sale. It was to be registered at the land recording office, it named the grantor and the grantee. But the city said it was not a sale. The law says that if the parties to the sale clearly state that what looks and smells like a deed is not a deed then it is not a deed. But if the grantee, the person buying the property, does not say anything, then it is valid sales transaction. As I read the agreement, it sold to the county a property interest in the land that was used for the dam. The situation was somewhat insane. The city said it was not a sale, but the county that was the grantee did not say anything. If the court ruled that it was a sale then the project was a denial of due process of law and should not go forward. Overall it is a complicated issue which courts often want to stay away from.

After the announcement that I was filing an action the Water Authority Executive Board went into emergency session and before I could file the action they filed their own action. They filed an action for a bond validation. They wanted the court to say that there was nothing wrong with what they were doing and the $31 million bond for the first part of the project was legal. I then filed my lawsuit and a motion to consolidate both cases. A hearing was held on the issue of whether to consolidate the cases.

Public relations wise, I looked like a joke. I was then 70 years of age, retired and had spent most of my legal career specializing in immigration law. As I said before, to most people, immigration lawyers are seen as the lowest level of lawyer often incapable of doing anything else other than chasing around illegal aliens. The headlines in the local paper read something like "Seventy year old immigration lawyer goes to court to stop the dam." At the press conference they asked if I had ever been in court before and I replied that often in Federal Court but seldom in State Court. I also told them I knew what I was doing. But they looked at me as if I was Don Quixote, an old man chasing windmills.

The first hearing was in the old court house in the center of town. It is a lovely brick court house that was built about the time of the Revolutionary War. Walking into the building I got a sense of history. Charlottesville is the town of three famous presidents: Thomas Jefferson, James Madison and James Monroe. I could feel their presence going through me as I walked in, especially Jefferson who at one time said that there should be a revolution in the country every 20 years. It was like his voice was whispering to me. "Go ahead and give them hell." Behind me were Bob, Jennifer, the press and a number of friends.

I filed the legal action in court and named as parties to the action the City of Charlottesville, the County of Albemarle and the Water Authority. Soon each of them replied to the complaint. The City once again said it was not a sale, the Water Authority said it was not a sale of real estate, the County, who is the grantor in the operating agreement that is to be filed with the land office, stated a number of reasons for the case to be dismissed but did not state that the agreement was not the equivalent of a sale. Until they said it was not a sale, the law assumed it was a sale. It is as crazy an issue as when I tell people that I threw my daughter out of the house and she tells everyone that I bought her a condo.

At the first hearing I introduced myself to Judge Higgins who was years ago an attorney for one of the large law firms. She was polite and asked if I was concerned about a possible conflict she may have being the Judge since she knew the parties so well. I replied that I was not concerned and believed she would be making the proper decisions. But there was something about the way she acted that led me to feel that she

                    STANTON BRAVERMAN

saw the case as a waste of her time. After all, this was a huge project for the city and the county, it was presented as though it was well thought out and the 70 year old immigration attorney standing in front of the bar was viewed as being incompetent to deal with the matter.

The hearing started and Kurt Krueger, the attorney for the Water Authority submitted about 10 inches of documents to support his claim for the bond validation. He did not explain what the documents related to but it was an impressive submission of evidence. After submitting them to the court and giving me a copy I looked at Kurt and read his facial expression to say to me, "Go ahead Mr. Immigration Lawyer, and have fun reading these documents." I realized that they were a decoy and to focus on them would be a waste of a huge amount of time. Besides I already had all the documents I needed. A quick look at them and it was clearly a pile of irrelevant stuff. Putting them aside I told the judge that I did not object to their introduction but reserved the right to change my position on their submission to the Court. Mr. Krueger then called to the witness chair the Executive Director of the Water Authority who sat there very pompously. Krueger asked what the documents related to and he stated they were copies of the environmental report, the report by the Army Corp of Engineers and various permits issued by the State of Virginia. Then it was my turn to cross-examine. At one point I wanted to cross- examine the Director of the Water Authority about a number of things but before I could ask any questions Judge Higgins said, "Mr. Braverman, limit your question to issues regarding the bond." It was clear that she was not the least bit interested in my legal claim that the project was in violation of due process of law. In a way it was very strange because none of the documents that were submitted as evidence pertained to the bond issue. They related to everything else besides the bond. It was a situation where I could not even ask any questions about these documents. As a result I was not able to do an effective cross examination. I had a suspicion that the case would go this way. Attorney friends of mine in Northern Virginia told me that the courts in Central Virginia were heavily influenced by local politics and that they would find a way to run me out of court as fast as they could.

The Judge at one point asked if I had any idea how the case would develop and what I intended to do. Since I had limited funds, I could not ask for depositions nor have expert witnesses. I planned to pursue the case as if it was limited to cross motions for summary judgement which means the focus would be on the law with an agreement to the facts. The Judge agreed with this approach and Krueger was happy that we were not going to look for stuff in the Authority's files. This is a trick I learned as an immigration attorney when filing an action against the government in Federal Court. A proper use of summary judgement procedures, if done right, it can be very effective.

STANTON BRAVERMAN

CHAPTER 13

FINDING THE NEEDLE IN THE HAYSTACK

T HE JUDGE AT that point continued the case for about four weeks to allow the parties to prepare for a formal argument. I went back to my office and I knew I had a lot more work to do. I got brushed off by the Judge over the scope of my cross examination and was sure that she would find my argument that there was an actual sale of the property to be frivolous and I had to find another way to deal with the matter. I read through a number of documents such as the Board minutes where the project was discussed, the various agreements, the press releases, the statute on water authority, and read various law review articles. I kept saying to myself that I am missing something. There has to be something more involved. Needed to know why Nestle was there, why the river issue? Maybe I'm just looking for a needle in a haystack.

And for the longest time I felt that I was going nowhere. I reread everything again and then the stroke of lightning that brings things together came into sharp focus. The Virginia Code, in three places, said that a water authority could issue bonds but only ones secured by revenue and no other collateral. The authorization document that was approved by the City Council casually stated that the $31 million loan would have as collateral three important things. The first was the water leases; the second was all the permits issued by government agencies; the third was the agreement between the city, the county and the water authority. Since most bonds of such size have some collateral which is there to assure the payments of interest and principle when they come due I had quickly ignored it. It was not until the third or fourth reading of the state code did I realize that they did not have the authority to put up any collateral besides revenue and yet they were putting up important items that were necessary to the continued operation of the water authority. And if the water authority could not pay its bills and the water system ended up in bankruptcy anyone who bought any of these at items at distressed prices would have de facto control of the water system. I was starting to get someplace. At first I thought the Authority had issued so many bonds that the banks were concerned that the project will go bankrupt. But I needed a clearer picture. Once more through the documents and I realized that the 5 ½ percent interest rate for the bond was very expensive for a water authority with a AA+ credit rating.

There was also something else that was strange about the interest rate. A properly prepared authorization for the bond should has stated, "an interest rate up to 5 1/2%" and not a fixed rate. I could not tell if this error was an oversight by the attorneys who prepared the documents or if it was deliberately done to push the project into bankruptcy. Because the law firm that worked on the documents was highly qualified in corporate finance, this led me to believe that it may not be a mistake.

That interest rate was actually a junk bond rate and would cost a lot of money and is for very risky loans. The interest rate at that time for the water authority with it superb bond rating should have been 3%. Reading further through the documents for the sixth or seventh time I realized that there were a lot of very strict conditions that would lead to a default. The bond could be considered in default if one of eight or nine events just happens to occur. And the final bit of information: It only required bond holders holding 10% of the bond to call for a default if any one of the eight conditions were met. Simple math says that 10% of $31 million is $3.1 million. If Nestle, through a group of investors bought only 10% of the bonds, they had the legal right to call for a default. That would send the water system into the bankruptcy court and then would allow for the court to order the sale of the assets that were put up for collateral. In effect, they could get control of a massive fresh water system for peanuts.

I called the attorney for the authority and told him that the bond could not include any collateral beyond revenue. This means that if the

     STANTON BRAVERMAN

Authority goes broke all the bondholders can do is to ask the court to order an increase in the water rates. But the city and the county get to keep their water system. Kurt said he was aware of this issue and was trying to work it out with the banks. That conversation got me excited. There was something really illegal in the project and I was on to it. It was clear that not only was the collateral issue illegal but I wondered if the Authority told the Board that it had a problem. After I reread one more time all the minutes of the Executive Board that pertained to the dam, I saw that there was one interesting comment. A special meeting was called by the attorney to discuss two major and important issues. After rereading the minutes for about the fourth time I realized they only discussed one important issue which did not relate to the improper use of collateral. There is nothing in the minutes that refers to the second important agenda item which in all probability was the collateral.

CHAPTER 14

NOTIFYING THE COURT OF THE ILLEGALITY

AFTER THINKING ABOUT the issue and the illegal attempt to put up collateral that that the law prohibited, and trying to figure out the best approach to bring this issue to the court, I developed a legal strategy. What appeared to be going is what I have seen lawyers for corporation do many times. They deliberately get sloppy about the work they do so they can take a fallback position of "Oh, it was nothing but an innocent mistake". Or they nibble on the sides between legality and illegality and then slowly they squirm out of any investigation that may happen. I felt that if I asked the attorney what the second issue was that was discussed in the meeting, I would probably get a reply like, "Stan, you have to understand that things were moving very fast and the minutes were done in a hurry. I am sorry about the problem. But we did discuss the issue of legal authority of putting up so much stuff for the collateral for the bond." It is typical corporate behavior which is done all the time and the job of many of the best law firms in the country is to explain to the client how this is done. They often do not give legal advice on how to avoid trouble. They know their clients will do anything and their job is to set it up so that when trouble does surface they can hide under a number of defenses. Deliberately I did not confront them on the incomplete minutes because it would only give them time to cover their asses.

Realizing that there were serious legal issues about the financial structure of the project I excitedly filed a motion with the Court to deny the bond validation to the Authority because they did not have the legal authority to include any collateral other than revenue. The motion stated that the State Code prohibited the use of such collateral in at least three places and that the Charter that was issued by the State clearly stated that they could not issue bonds with collateral other than revenue. After filing this I knew I had a strong legal issue to pursue and it was an issue that the water authority, Kurt and the Court could not duck. They had to deal with it.

About two weeks later we were back in court. I greeted the opposition with a smile and friendly conversation. One of them told me that I was messing with a major project that had been cleared all the way to the state capital. A lot of important people were interested in the dam and I was standing in its way. That was interesting news because it showed that there was possibly a lot of shenanigans and high level political activity behind what was now appearing to be an illegal project.

As we walked into court and going over everything in my mind one more time I realized that the Authority had not submitted a rebuttal to my motion to deny the bond since it exceeded their authority and because it was prohibited in three places in the State Code. In addition, collateral is only required by the banks or investors when the project is weak and it looks like there is a need to assure payment. This may exist when the Water Authority has issued too many bonds and appears to be spending beyond reasonable limits. The 5% junk bond interest rate suggested that the Water Authority had in fact borrowed too much and it had a bad credit rating. The day before I went through the documents and quickly verified that the Authority has an AA+ rating which is far from junk bond status. Something was not right. Whatever the shenanigans were, the people who greeted me as I walked into court were telling me that the governor was involved.

The issues of relationship between the need for collateral works versus the procedure for correcting a default if there is no collateral kept going through my head. If the only collateral for the bond is revenue and in the event the Authority cannot pay its bills then the only thing the bank can do is go into court and file a Mandamus action against that Authority and have the court order that they raise water rates to pay for the debt service for the bond. It can do nothing more and while the court may require an increase in water rates the city gets to keep control over its water authority. Basically the statutory limitation on the use of collateral put a limit on the amount of money that the Authority could borrow, but it appeared that the RWSA was nowhere near its borrowing limit and the need for the collateral made no sense. In simple day to day terms, imagine a man's brother comes to him to co-sign a note for a new car. The brother says that the bank wants him to co-sign. But a review of the brother's financial record shows that he earns a lot of money and does not owe anyone anything. In that case there is no need for the person to co-sign. Any person with any financial background would quickly realize that there was a strong possibility that the way the project was structured and financed the water authority could go bankrupt but not because the authority had owed too much money. It was an oversized project that did not have a population base to support it and at a junk bond interest rate. As all of this ran through my head and hearing the man outside the court saying that there were a lot of important people behind this project and I was getting in their way along with the manner in which the Judge limited the cross examination of the Executive Director suggest that something improper and illegal was going on. Maybe many people within the state government were actually behind this insane project. It smelled so bad that for a moment I thought maybe the Judge was in on the deal. All of these issues were floating through my head as I walked into Court.

As I was walking in, Jennifer said, "Stan, you forgot to shine your shoes." What else do you expect a wife to say when she sees her husband going into court? "Forget the shoes; I need to get my eye glasses cleaned." A couple of people in the court looked at me as to why my glasses were dirty and I told them my eyelashes were too long. A couple of the ladies looked at me and commented "Why do I not have that problem?" Jennifer, looked at them and commented, "I just do not understand my husband. I had to remind him to shave this morning. His suit is wrinkled and he needs to shine his shoes." But Jennifer did not understand that most of this behavior is deliberate. I love being a Colombo-type character who is completely disheveled. It always puts the opposition at ease and they never see what is coming at them until it is too late. As I sat down at the assigned table in the courtroom and looked across to the other side, I saw four lawyers from the best law firm in the state, wearing nice suits and all looking at me as if they were going to eat me alive. One of the attorneys was the law firm's expert on municipal bonds. Another attorney was a senior litigator for the firm. I assume the collective fee they were charging the authority was well over $2,000 an hour. In addition to that there were charges for legal research that associates have to do, paralegal fees and other expenses. If I dragged the case out for a while I figure I could bankrupt that Authority on legal fees, but since I was trying to save it from bankruptcy I wanted to shortcut the issue in court, but get it resolved in my favor.

CHAPTER 15

HEARING ON THE MERITS

AN ATTORNEY GOING into court to fight for his client is similar to a boxer going into a boxing match. All the preparation and all the advice that is worked on before the fight often is not going to work and the boxer has to develop his own strategy as the fight goes on. After many years of being a lawyer and in many different types of courts I was well aware that anything can happen in court and I need to be prepared for it (such as the ten inches of irrelevant documents they submitted as evidence.) They will throw punches and I need to duck them; they will fake punches and I need to ignore them, they will cry "foul" and I need to quickly respond. But after 40 years of playing this game what I saw in court that day was shocking.

The hearing began; it was round one. The issue was my original argument that the project as approved by the city was in violation of law. It was a very complicated argument and I knew that Judges often have problems with complicated issues, especially when there is a lot of pressure on them about the case. As expected the Judge quickly denied my argument and then went into the issue of the bond validation. And that is when I started fighting back.

"Your Honor, the Court cannot validate or approve the bond because it includes collateral that the state code says they cannot do as I point out in by motion and supporting legal brief. Collateral is an important aspect of any financing and the state legislature has clearly stated that water authorities and systems are very important to the local communities and cannot be jeopardized by having them put up as collateral. It is also a limitation on the amount of borrowing they can do and that limitation is when they reach the point that their financial structure is weak and they have to include excessive collateral to get financing. If they need the collateral for the bond then it is clear that they are not operating the Water Authority as it is, by law, to operate."

Then the lawyer for the government got up and told the Judge he would like to withdraw the issue of the collateral from the validation process. His position was that it was not part of the process for approval of a bond.

My response to that comment was that the State code that set up the bond validation process clearly said that the court SHALL determine the appropriateness of the collateral. If the authority wished to withdraw the issue of collateral from the bond they are in effect asking the court to deny the right to sell the bond. When I said this the Judge quickly looked at a copy of the statute that was in front of her and she clearly understood that they could not remove it. The bond and the collateral issue were a package. That is the way the State Code mandated it.

The argument went back and forth and I refused to give up on the issue. I remember the attorney telling the Judge he was only asking the court to approve something that was done 21 times before. I let that comment slide by me rather than pointing out that the Authority has admitted to violation of the State Code 21 times in the past. While the statement was true, in the past the bond authorizations had put up as collateral relatively small amounts of money that set aside for special needs. They were not a significant factor for anyone to complain about even though they were in clear violation of their written legal authority. That statement "21 times" rang through my head. The feeling was that at the Executive Board Meeting for two important issues, of which only one issue was recorded, the attorney may have told the Board that there was an illegal issue regarding the bond but since they had already done it 21 times before it seemed to be irrelevant. It became obvious that the 21 times before was the fall back position in the event "the shit hit the fan" as we used to describe such situations back in Philly.

There was the 21 times thing, the poorly worded statement on the interest rate, an interest rate that was too expensive, the people at the door as I walked in telling me that the project has been cleared through Richmond. It was one pile of shit and I was wondering what was coming next.

CHAPTER 16

CHAOS IN COURT

THEN THE STRANGEST thing happened, something I had never seen in court. The one lawyer, who they told me was their senior litigator, calmly handed the judge a document without showing it to me. The Judge took the paper and either did not notice that I did not get a copy of the document, which is always done in court or she deliberately overlooked the failure to give a copy to me. I asked the attorney what he had just given the Judge and he replied in a very sarcastic tone, "What is it, Mr. Braverman, that you do not understand?" I then looked up and realized whatever the document was, it was in front of the Judge and she had a pen in her hands and it appeared that she was about to sign it. And then I felt as if the Judge and the others were just trying to screw around with me. This analysis may have been right or wrong, it did not matter. What was happening was clearly out of order; since the judge had previously treated me shabbily, I was convinced that the Judge was working with the Authority lawyers to kick me out of court. I needed to resort to tough unorthodox tactics or else they were about to eat me alive. I quickly spoke out loud and clear. What I said was not for the Judge but for the court reporter because I wanted the record to clearly show this crude behavior.

"Your Honor, I want the record to reflect that the attorney for the authority has given you a document for you to sign and he has not shown it to me. I suspect that the document is a proposed final order and if it is, and if the order includes any provision for any collateral other than revenue, I will run this order down to Richmond as fast as I can." The reference to Richmond, the State Capital, clearly meant that I would quickly file an appeal of a decision that was clearly wrong and had no legal authority behind it. The appeal of the order which she signed would be a reflection of her ability as a Judge that would be heard by the court.

I learned years ago that when Judges go nuts, and at times they do so, the best way to deal with it is to get the behavior on the record and then appeal. Most times it will bring the judge back to reality and the nonsense ends. This is exactly what happened. Judge Higgins threw down her pen, jumped out of her chair and started to leave the courtroom. As she left she instructed the staff to give me a copy of the document. While my eyes were focused on the Judge, Jennifer later told me that immediately after I made this statement the four attorneys and their clients and others who were supporting the project got into a huddle and acted as if the proceedings were getting away from them. I did not notice this because I was then reading the document which, as I suspected, was a proposed order and it allowed all the collateral that they said was needed to get the financing and it was clearly illegal. I do not know what the judge was thinking but it appeared to me that she was willing to sign the order so long as I was not prepared to appeal it. But if it was appealed to the State Supreme Court then her name would go with it and it was clearly an illegal act and that the Authority was not entitled to the order.

About five minutes later she came back into court and asked me what I had to say about the proposed order. I quickly said I would not agree to it. And then she told us to compromise. As soon as she said that I realized I found a way to get the matter out of the hands of the State of Virginia and into the Federal system. I was just getting continually beaten up by the State of Virginia because of the political pressure for the project. There was a need to argue the issues someplace else. There were three important things they wanted for collateral. One was the working agreement which was the operational authority to run the system. In that document was a provision for all the water leases for the water rights the city owned. They also wanted all the permits and the water leases. But the water leases were in the agreement and if the agreement was withdrawn then it could be argued that the leases went with it. Since there was not a separate agreement for the water leases then a reasonable argument could be made that if the order said they had the leases, but did not have the agreement, they really did not have it. The thought quickly went through my brain and I felt that if the issue went to Richmond anything could happen. I had at this point almost beaten myself to death learning the law of municipal bond financing, water rights, the law of water authorities and the permit process. I was totally exhausted and not prepared for a "Good Ole Boy" attack that would be waiting for me in Richmond.

I looked up at the Judge and said, "They can have the water leases, and they have to take out everything else." They quickly agreed to that compromise and we changed the language of the order and signed it. The lawyer for the authority was very happy and he later told me he got what he wanted. Everyone in the court looked at me as if I was nuts and wanted to know why I agreed to the compromise. But I was exhausted and felt it was for the best and I had a secret strategy to follow up on.

          STANTON BRAVERMAN

CHAPTER 17

BOB FENWICK GOES TO BAT FOR THE CITY

T HERE WAS ACTUALLY more to the court scene that focused on the need and court approval of the bond. A municipal bond validation hearing actually involves everyone who lives or is employed or owns property in the city and the county. They water authority will file the case with the local state court: then service of process is obtained by advertising in local newspapers. This tells them that the authority plans to issue a bond and if they have an issue to notify the court. Since this type of procedure is against the whole community and anyone can object, my friend, the general contractor for the addition to the house, the person who got me all upset about Ragged Mountain, Bob Fenwick, filed a notice with the Court and appeared in Court with me to object. Bob was doing his thing to go to bat for the city. At least he could say something to the Judge. At the hearing the Judge was confused as to why he was there and when I pointed out to her the legality of it and his right to be heard she seemed to understand and did comment that at some point he would have the right to speak. But in the chaos of court hearing she forgot to do this and Bob never got a chance to speak. But Bob did not agree with the order that the Judge signed so he filed an appeal to the State Supreme Court. This became an important issue in the city press but soon the case was dismissed by the Court because he failed to serve a copy of the appeal to a couple of people. While Bob was bothered by the denial of his appeal for a technical reason, it confirmed to me that the political pressure for the project was very strong in Richmond because the court could have easily taken the case on its own motion, especially because it dealt with an issue of public health and safety. But the Supreme Court refused to do so and the appeal was dismissed. Here was an issue where the legislature had said three times that such collateral is clearly not in the public interest and the failure of the court to take it only confirmed my paranoid thinking.

The way in which the validation process works is an example of how easy it is for corporate America to screw everyone. It relies on an important doctrine in law of re judicata. This doctrine says that if you are a party to a legal action and it is decided and a final order is signed by the judge then all persons who were involved in the matter are stopped from pursuing the issue. It is an effort to get finality to a decision. The concept itself is a good one because it keeps people from arguing the same issue over and over again. But the way it works in a bond hearing is that the announcement in the paper makes everyone a party, and when the judge signs the order then everyone has to accept it as a final decision. If the judge signed the order as they presented it to her and I did not appeal, that order would be binding on everyone in the city even though most people have no idea that they have been sued. Before the final hearing on the bond a number of people asked what they could do to help and I told them to write a letter to the court saying that they opposed the building of the dam. A number of people did this and some of them besides Bob appeared in court. They had all been sued and because the public seldom, if ever, responds to such notices in the paper, the Judge had no idea on how to let them proceed.

The Banks and investment companies that will promote and sell the bonds once approved have strong interests in the bond validation process. They want reasonable assurance that the bond meets all of the technicalities of the State Law and that the bond when issued will not later be declared by a court to be illegally promoted and sold. The way it generally works is similar to a "friendly suit." That happens when two or more parties reach an agreement about a legal issue and they need a court to approve it. One side will sue the other and they both appear in court to advise the court that it is a friendly suit. They will give the Judge a proposed order that both sides have agreed to, the Judge will review it to see if it appears to be justified, and then sign it. It is often nothing more than a quick trip to the court on a motion calendar day. Normally

STANTON BRAVERMAN

with a bond validation it is assumed that the local government has followed the law and has properly authorized the issuance of the bond. With probably all bond validation hearings the parties are in agreement and it is quickly approved by the court. The problem with the bond for Ragged Mountain is that the local community that promoted the project was not concerned about whether or not it was illegal or legal because they felt that no one would attack the bond in court and that is what made it legal. I have been a resident of Virginia and a member of the Bar Association since 1986 and it appalls me that the State code can be so carelessly ignored, at least in Central Virginia.

CHAPTER 18

TAKING THE CASE TO THE FEDERAL GOVERNMENT

WHILE IT APPEARED to everyone that I lost the case I was not through with the matter. I just wanted to get it out of the State government. After the court hearing I returned to my office and turned on the computer and went to the web site of the Security and Exchange Commission in Washington DC. This agency, among other duties, investigates and prosecutes security frauds. I knew the Authority had to file with the appropriate agency and a formal notice of the bond and its provisions would say that the water leases were included in the collateral. Once I got to the SEC web site I looked for the section to report security fraud and when I found it I advised the agency to be on the lookout for this filing. I advised the SEC that there would be a provision in the bond that said that the water leases were part of the collateral for the loan. I also advised that this was not correct even though the court order said they could have the leases. The argument focused on the Dillon rule which is strictly followed in Virginia. This rule says that a state agency can only do something if they have the clear authority to do it. If there is any ambiguity on that authority, it is assumed that they cannot do it.

I advised the SEC that the leases were in the operational agreement and that document was withdrawn from the list of items to be collateralized. Since there was not a separate document that included the leases they had to put back the agreement – which was not done. Second, the Code for the State of Virginia stated clearly in three places that the authority cannot issue a bond with collateral other than revenue and that the operating charter of the authority limited bond collateral to only revenue. In effect, it was not clear that they had the authority to include leases as collateral and because Virginia follows the Dillon rule the only conclusion is that they do not have the authority. The complaint was filed, Ragged Mountain was behind me and that the SEC would take care of the problem.

CHAPTER 19

VICTORY

MONTHS LATER THE bond had yet been issued and the City Council was advised that everything was going OK but things had to be worked out. Then one day the bond was issued and they got the $31 million. About a month later, one member of the City Council asked me if the leases were put up for collateral and I said I would check it out. The Council member had previously asked the Authority for this information on two different occasions. The first answer was "we have complied with the Court order." The second time the question was asked they replied "The information is in the relevant documents." Clearly they were non responsive to the question.

I called the attorney and asked him the same question and I got the same type of nonresponsive answer which I refused to accept. "Listen carefully, I am prepared to go back to court with a declaratory judgement action to get a clear answer to the question."

"Braverman, you accepted the order as a final order and you cannot reopen it."

"I still have the right to bring an action to determine if you are complying with the order and if I do so I will bring in the bank since they are the trustee on the bonds and once they are served, your client will never get them to cooperate with you on the next loan. Banks hate to be dragged into court."

There was a pause and then the Attorney said. "Stan, you know what the SEC did. We had to take out the water leases as collateral."

I thanked him for the conversation and then called the Council member and told that the only collateral on the bond is revenue. Which meant that if the project fails then all the bond holders can do is have the court order an increase in water rates. There is one more fascinating issue. When the bond was sold the interest rate was at about 3% rather than the 5% that the Board had agreed to. This is a two percent reduction in the interest rate and for a $31 million bond this amounts to about $620,000 a year in savings. Here is a situation where most of the collateral is removed and the interest rate goes down. Normal financial behavior is when with most of the collateral removed the rate should be going up. This lower interest rate only confirmed my suspicions that shenanigans were at work.

About a week after the last phone call with the attorney I got an unexpected email from the SEC advising me that the registration notification for the bond could be found on the internet. I checked the site and there on page 7 was a statement that said "the only collateral for the bond was revenue and to include any other collateral was illegal in Virginia". The SEC did its job. I do not know how they did it. Maybe they send a simple letter to the authority advising them of the issue and that encouraged them to change things. Or it could have been that they told the Authority that there was a serious issue with security fraud that they were prepared to investigate. Actually I did not care how they did it. I then sent a copy of the email to all the members of the City Council, the City Attorney and to Bob Fenwick and then declared victory. In the end Colombo won his case. Yet it allowed the Authority to walk away without embarrassment and they never publicly stated that they had a problem with the SEC. If you ask them how the case worked out they will say that they got the dam built. But whoever was behind the scene that was trying to bankrupt the water system does not appear to be around anymore. I suspect it was Nestle who was trying to make a grab for the system but at this point I cannot prove it. Maybe one day the missing pieces to the puzzle will become public. But Nestle is still going through America trying to get fresh water for its bottling operations any way it can. I do not hold it against them because fresh water is a commodity that is ever decreasing in availability. Actually at the current time, fresh bottled water often sells for a higher price than gasoline. Because clear fresh water is quickly becoming a commodity like oil or gold Corporate America will continue to try to find ways to own it and then monopolize the market.

Yet, private ownership of water systems has serious public policy concerns. First, water right issues continuously evolve and the allocation of fresh water is always changing. Second, the people need water as much as they need fresh air and oxygen. If a water system is privatized it is possible that the owners will raise the cost to monopolistic levels. This actually happened in the Charlottesville area and has seriously affected the price of real estate. Outside of the city is an area known as Lake Monticello. In that community a private company owns the water system and they have high prices for the water. I have met people who live in the community and they have told me that a family of four people will be paying about $200 a month for water. That is to be compared to the $40 a month charge that we pay RWSA each month for fresh water and wastewater treatment. Humans can become pigs when it comes to finding oil or gold. They lose their sense of morality and all they think of is the huge profits they can make once they get it. The same is quickly becoming true with fresh water. Today it is a huge business. At most stadiums when baseball games or football games are played, bottled fresh water is the number one drink that people buy. It outsells Coke, Pepsi or any other sugar drink. It sells for the same price, yet its ingredients often are basic – just water with no additives and the profit margin is huge. Nestle makes a lot of money from the sale of bottled water and it appears from what is found on the internet about the company, they want to grab more and more of the market and at the same time obtain the basic ingredient (water) at lower costs.

When they rewrote the Code a few years ago, the State of Virginia was very much aware of this problem and tried to deal with it by writing in three places that for a bond issued by a water authority the only collateral for their bonds is revenue. All the bond holders can do, if the system goes broke, is to go to court and ask the court to increase the cost of the water to the customer. The end result is that the people get to keep their water system. The bond market is not asking for the water authority to provide any collateral because they know that they will be paid. This was clearly true with the $31 million bond proposed by RWSA. The bond sold at a low price without the collateral. The banks apparently never told the Authority that the collateral was necessary.

     STANTON BRAVERMAN

From a financial point of view it was not necessary. Then why was it there? RWSA has yet to give an answer to this question and it looks like someone wanted to see the system fail and go into bankruptcy. Numerous emails were sent to the City Council and the City Attorney advising them that the way the bond was structured was illegal and that none of the notes of any of the Executive Board meetings discuss this issue.

I assume that after the SEC intervention that lawyers for the Authority had rewritten the documents and then advised the Board that they could only include revenue as collateral and that the use of anything else was illegal. But at the time of the court case the attorneys failed to officially advise the City, the County and the water authority that it would be illegal to include such collateral. Yet an attorney has the responsibility to tell his client that the activity is illegal. Following the notice received from the SEC that the only collateral was revenue could be used I send numerous emails to the City Council advising for them to investigate why they were not properly notified. There were no replies to these emails and it can be assumed that their inactivity suggests that they were fully aware of the shenanigans. Instead they do what all haughty people do and will never admit to any mistake. They just pretend that nothing ever happened and go on to the next fiasco.

In the end Charlottesville and the county will keep control over the water authority. It will not be sold at a bankruptcy auction and if the project fails then water rates will go up a few dollars every month and not to the high levels that are paid by residents of Lake Monticello. The decrease in the interest rate by two percent will save the area millions of dollars that can be used for maintaining schools, building bridges and other needed projects.

CHAPTER 20

CORPORATE BEHAVIOR AND RAGGED MOUNTAIN

THE MOTTO OF Corporate America is when the law stands in your way, then find a way to change it. They will send their lobbyists to Richmond when the legislature is in session and push for small changes here and there and over time they will try to grab all of it. They do this because they are always prospecting for gold and now fresh water is in that arena. The fear is one day they will get the legislature to change the law to allow for the water authorities to include major assets as collateral. In recent years the primary objective of Corporate America is to figure out a way to get private enterprise to take over more and more the role of government. While the Constitution says that one of the powers of the US government is to provide a postal system, there are many companies who want to do this job. The Constitution allows for the government to establish a highway system but many people are pushing for privately run toll roads. The healthcare system in the US is a complete mess because many companies argue that health insurance companies should be privately owned and allowed to compete against each other rather than allowing for a single payer system that has been proved to be much more effective in almost every other developed country. Corporate America has found an easy way to do it. They have huge amounts of money and can afford to hire an army of lobbyists to walk the halls of Congress and State legislatures to get them to change laws and regulations that allow for them to get more and more. They are never satisfied with what they have.

Historically, Corporate America was made up of exciting organizations. They built steel mills, railroads, and factories: most people agreed that what was good for them was good for the United States. I remember as a child watching television, there was one advertisement that said it all. It was a Merrill Lynch ad. They are a brokerage firm and the ad said that they made their money the hard way - they earned it. And people believed it. Today Corporate American earns its money the easy way by hiring lobbyists to change laws and regulations so they can increase their profit margins by raising costs, creating monopolies or by getting government subsidies. Lobbyists have become so effective that the rate of return on money spent on lobbyists is often a 1000 to 1. That means that for every dollar spent for a lobbyist they expect to get a $1000 back.

This was pointed out in Howard Zinn's book, People's History of America. He writes about the milk industry which was afraid that they would lose a government subsidy. The industry pooled their resources, and with $500,000, hired lobbyists to go to Congress. In the end they kept their subsidy and got an increase that amounted to about $500 millions. If you do the math, the rate of return was 1000 to 1.

One day Corporate America will hire lobbyists to walk into the halls of the state Capital with a sob story about how the collateral restriction on the water authority loans is making it difficult for them. They'll convince the legislature to rewrite the state code and then encourage local water authorities to put up water systems for collateral for bonds. The projects will be designed to fail and the company will take them over and they will raise the water rates to atrocious levels.

One more note about the hunt for clear fresh water by corporations. One day when I got to the cabin, there was a strange notice attached to the door. It was from the Piedmont Environmental Council and Trout Unlimited which had previously been associated with the Nations Conservancy and the Nestle Foundation over the Moormon River and Ragged Mountain. The notice advised that they were disturbed that it was necessary to ford across the Robinson River to get to our property and that it would be better for us to build a culvert across the river. This would assure that the trout would be able to safely migrate up the river. They were prepared to assist in such in building a culvert across the river. I investigated the issue and found that there were plenty of brook trout in the river and they were not threatened. Second, while they are willing to provide a lot of the financing for the project they would probably require that I transfer to them any water rights I have in the river as it cascades through our property. Again the project made no sense. The trout were doing fine as it was and it was not necessary to change things. I sent an email back to the originator of the notice and told them that they had no authorization to enter my property and if they came back I would call the sheriff to have them arrested for criminal trespassing. They scare me because for about 800 feet we own both sides of the Robinson River which is a series of small cascading falls that if cleared out in spots would be a fantastic trout fishing spot for the rich. If they grabbed the water rights the next thing that would happen is that they would be selling fishing rights for a day for price above the $185 that they charge down river. We prefer to keep the shore line overgrown the way nature wants it to be and let the brook trout live in peace.

There were two curious incidents that happened during the Ragged Mountain legal action that may or may not be related to the dam. The first incident relates to a phone message that was on the office answering machine. It was the sexy voice of a woman, "Hi, I am Rebecca, and I am interested in what immigration attorneys do. Can I meet with you sometime so you can explain it to me?" Everyone laughed at the message. The question was who is Rebecca? Was she really interested in an immigration law office or was she calling for some other sinister purpose? At times there would be messages from women with sexy voices asking if the office can get a green card for a boyfriend, but never a call as vague as this. Jennifer wanted me to call her back and everyone else thought she was a call girl on a mission to compromise me because of the court case that was still going on.

Jennifer kept pushing for me to call. But we told her that if she was trying to compromise me and if I call her back I would end up in bed with her, let her take the pictures and when they show me the pictures to convince me to drop the case, I would then have them arrested for extortion. But I would have to go that far and Jennifer would have to agree to it, which she refused to do. The message from Rebecca stayed on the answering machine and at times it would be played back for friends to get their comments. This went on for about six months and Jennifer would still occasionally ask that we call her back. One day we did call her back and found the telephone number had been discontinued. We then deleted the message.

The reason for being suspicious about the purpose of the call is that over the 40 years of being an attorney on a number of important issues there have been other women who appeared to be trying to compromise me. But these stories are for another book.

The second incident was scary. One day I was leaving our house in Charlottesville to go to the mountain house using the back roads and not along the major road, Route 29, that was the normal route. While this route was about 7 miles longer it was through beautiful winding country roads that went past farms, cattle grazing in fields. There was never any traffic and it was a great way to brush off the frustration of inner city living. Within two blocks after leaving the office, looking out the rear view mirror I saw an SUV and four men. They followed rather closely. About three miles later they were still behind the car. They closely followed for 20 miles to Barboursville and then turned with me on to route 33 and then back on to route 20, which went to Orange, Virginia. At Summerset, the route calls for a turn on to route 231. Looking in the mirror, I saw that they were still there. It is 12 miles to Madison and they stayed close behind most of the way. As we approached Pratt it was time to do something. I put the gas pedal to the floor and the car was going far above the speed limit and they were still behind me. But at that point Route 231 has a lot of difficult curves and at the speed the car was going, only a driver who knew the road could safely stay on the roadway. They stayed closely behind for about a half mile and then abruptly they turned on to a side street. I later told Bob about the incident and he cautioned me to be careful. While it was an uncomfortable ride there never appeared to be any real danger. It was at best an effort to intimidate me and maybe to send me a subtle message that I should forget about Ragged Mountain. If the men in the SUV were actually trying to cause physical harm they could have tried it anywhere along the route and they did not. But then again it just could have been four men in suits driving an SUV going to one the farms in the area owned by the super-rich.

CHAPTER 21

THE COUNCIL TRIES TO PLACATE BELMONT

BY THIS TIME we had already humiliated the City Council over the noise issue in Belmont and shock them up over Ragged Mountain where they were caught trying to pull a fast one on the local population. With Ragged Mountain behind me at least the town realized that I could litigate and litigators are always scary to a businessman because they can take him to court and drag the case out until he is bankrupt. I felt that the City government would start to grow up and limit their funny stuff to that which was legal and not going ahead and doing what they want because there was no one in the town who could take them to court. But haughty politicians are slow learners and I was soon to find other fights waiting for me.

Things started to get better in Charlottesville. The Council was starting to notice Belmont because it held a neighborhood meeting at the Clark Elementary School and they talked about all the things that they planned to do for the community. But it was a ridiculous meeting because they said that they were concerned about the neighborhood and wanted to help, but they could not agree on anything. One of the issues pertained to what some of us refer to as the Jim Baldi Memorial Park. After Bel Rio closed the city did some changes in downtown Belmont; none of them made any sense. The sidewalk in front of what was Bel Rio was enlarged; they changed the way the curbs flowed on Hinton Street to where they protruded into the street and created a traffic hazard. They told us that the curbs would get drivers to slow down when they got to Downtown Belmont. These new curbs reduced the number of parking places on the block and as far as slowing down the traffic, it never happened and almost everyone has run over them at one time or another. They did brick up the enlarged sidewalk and said they were going to put benches there which they never did. . They got the bricks by tearing up the lovely bricked pedestrian lane that allowed people to cross the street. In their place, they put down painted zebra lines which do not match the character of the old brick walkways. At the meeting we asked why the plaza was still empty of anything. It was just a bunch of bricks. One of the government officials at the meeting said that they were looking at giant flower pots that they could put a small tree into. They think they found them in the city warehouse. As I told Bob Fenwick, who was now on the Council, after the meeting, "It was a nice bag of promises but do you realize the only thing they are giving us is a couple of recycled flower pots?" Bob laughed but said that he could only do so much because he was only one vote out of five.

Then there is the issue of the Belmont Bridge. When I first arrived in the town, which is over ten years ago, there was a public hearing about the design of the new bridge that goes over the railroad tracks and connects Belmont with the center of the city. According to the city officials at the meeting, the state government said that the bridge is old and dangerous and has to be replaced. I went to the meeting and met with the engineering firm that was paid a lot of money to design the bridge. It looked like an exciting project. They told us that the construction project would take maybe about two years but they would keep open at least one lane in each direction. They said they could do it in a lot less time if they could close off the bridge. But the bridge issue then went silent. Nothing was heard about when construction would begin. Then the next year the local paper announced that there was a contest of the architectural students as to which student could come up with the best plan for a new bridge. All the money they spent in design specification and engineering studies seemed to disappear. A young student won the contest by completely taking down the bridge and having railroad gates come up and down. The next year another engineering design firm got a contract to do exactly what the first firm did. Announcements were made about hearings to discuss the new bridge and few of us went. We were starting to realize that the bridge, which the state government said was dangerous, would never get replaced. There were announcements in the paper again about the bridge and again the subject just went silent for a year and then it was announced that the second firm that did the re-design work closed down and they do not know where all the drawings went. At the current time there are no plans to build the bridge; one sidewalk is closed off because the concrete is so bad they cannot repair it. If you are under the bridge where there is some public parking and look up, a person will see a lot of plywood carefully strapped to the under part of the concrete road. The only thing not holding up the bridge is duct tape and bubble gum. The City Council each year puts the new bridge into the budget and then gets a lot of people thinking it will get done. But the money is never appropriated and the issue is forgotten for another year. the In the meantime the Belmont neighborhood has continued to develop and many homes have been remodeled. The price of real estate has greatly increased and along with it so have the assessed values. The house we remodeled was originally assessed for $130,000 and is now assessed for $430,000. The neighborhood is now making a strong positive contribution to the city treasury but the City Council and many of the government officials still ignore Belmont. At recent Council meetings there are discussions about building new bridges in other parts of the town with Bob arguing that they first have to take care of the current infrastructure. Some of the local residents are suggesting that we petition the city and the county to allow Belmont to withdraw from the city and join the surrounding county. If the neighborhood loses its bridge it will cut us off from the city and the only direction we can go is into the county.

Then comes the issue of the rezoning application for Lyman Street. This has to be the most ridiculous application for zoning that was ever presented to any city council. Lyman Street is at the end of Douglas Ave, the street where we live. It is adjacent to the railroad yard. At that corner is a small lot that runs along the tracks. It is about 40 feet wide and about 100 feet long. It was all woods in the back along the tracks and open grass along Layman Street. The developer who submitted the application to change the zoning had previously built a nice condo

     STANTON BRAVERMAN

apartment complex that was adjacent to this lot. But the complex was much larger than this small lot. For years no one saw any value in the lot. There were two major issues with it. First, it was too small for housing because there was not enough set back as required by the city code. The second was that all streets around Lyman Street already were handling more traffic than they could. They were small streets that were built well over a 100 years ago when people went around primarily by walking. The outlet for the lot went through a nice residential neighborhood. The developer somehow bought the property from the railroad and then submitted an application for it to be rezoned "Downtown Extended'" That was the classification for the buildings on the other side of the tracks where it was mostly a commercial sector. At first, he proposed a multi story office building and when the neighborhood strongly objected to that idea he tried to sweeten the project to partial residential and partial commercial. He said it would be a yoga studio and office building. But no one came forward to say that they were prepared to run such a studio at that location and I doubt they would because customers would find it difficult to get through to the building because of the very narrow streets.

So far this was normal builder nonsense, but soon we found the insanity of the application. The builder was broke. He lost all his money with the housing crash and he did not have the funds to build what he was proposing. He even admitted it and said that if he got the rezoning he would sell the land to another builder who would then decide what to do with the property. What he wanted was to make a quick dollar, which he needed, at the expense of the surrounding community. While this seemed to me to be absurd, it seems to be normal business in Charlottesville where a lot of money is spent for dumb things such as constantly redesigning the adjacent bridge. In Charlottesville this is called neighborhood planning and I call it chaos. It also showed the total lack of interest in the Belmont community. The idea that they will assist a local developer in getting financially back on his feet by denigrating a nice residential neighborhood is appalling without any idea what would be done with the property. The city government would not consider such an action in any other part of town. But the rezoning would be in

Belmont and that is a section where the poor folks and ignorant folks live. The zoning board approved the project with a four to one vote.

The way the zoning application was processed through the city government was that it was submitted to the Neighborhood Planning Office which also oversees the zoning. There was a public hearing at the board and everyone objected to it. The Board was not prepared for such opposition to the application and started to look for a way to continue the matter. It was amazing about how they went about doing it. During the public meeting with everyone objecting to it the members of the board said they needed to find old documents regarding the rezoning of the property about 50 years ago. They admitted that they could not find the documents but they adjourned to take another look. It was never clear why they needed these documents. After adjourning to look for unknown documents they met in secret and approved the application. They never disclosed if they found the documents. When the Board was asked why they did not hold another public meeting they stated that the public had already expressed their views. This to me was a closed door decision. By now everyone in the neighborhood was upset. Belmont had turned the corner and many of the residents were professionals who wanted to work and live in the city. The City Council and the NPO never noticed this trend and continued to see Belmont as a waste land for poor people. The next stop for the rezoning application was the City Council and at that point things got confusing. I feel the Council realized they had a problem because Stan Braverman said he was prepared to go to court on the issue. I met with Bob Fenwick who was feeling me out on the issue and I told him I would clearly go to court. The fact that the project is absurd – it was a rezoning application for a project that did not exist and the Zoning Board is not there for phantom projects - the fact that they did it in closed door meeting showed it was in violation of due process requirements and was serious grounds for filing an action in court. Bob indicated to me that the majority of the Council was prepared to approve and that I could go to court if I wanted to.

I told Bob, "Go back to the Council and tell them that if they approve the rezoning I will not only go to court and I know I will win, but I will announce my candidacy for a seat on the Council in the next election. I believe Kathy Galvin is up for re-election and it will be fun to run against her. She ran for election last time because she stood for "Green" and then proceeded to vote to destroy the old forests at Ragged Mountain. Now it appears she wants to take down the trees along the railroad tracks. It seems to me that when she talks about green stuff she is referring to the color of money and not anything that is living. I do not know if Bob took me seriously or not. One of the neighbors who is active with the community organization told me that the Council had suddenly put the issue to the end of a meeting and approved the rezoning without notifying the public about it being on the agenda. We do not know exactly what happened, but it was put back on the agenda for the next meeting. Everyone sent emails to the council objecting to the plan. I sent to them an email that said I would be there but everything I had to say was already said and I was just looking for a way to go into court.

A couple of days before the council meeting all the members of the council came to Lyman Street and walked around and they saw the narrow streets, the nice residential neighborhood. They did not let on what they intended to do. Two days later at the hearing Christine, our neighbor who was now active with the Belmont Carlton Neighborhood Committee (which Jim Baldi no longer controlled,) volunteered to speak for all of us because the mayor said he would allow only one person to speak for the community. Before speaking Christine reviewed the city code and realized that it said that "Downtown extended" zoning classification can only be used where there is an easy access to a commercial road network. This did not exist with this application for Lyman Street. At the meeting Christine did a great job in speaking for all of us and then the Neighborhood Planning Office representative spoke.. He told the Council that his office recommended approval. It was strange in that the Planning Office, which has responsibility for zoning issue and are the experts on zoning regulations, did not notice that the rezoning was in violation of the city code. Instead it was brought out by Kathy Galvin who spoke to us on behalf of the Council. She pointed out that the application did not conform to the zoning requirements and that the recommended change was not proper for the neighborhood. She made a nice presentation about the absurdity of the zoning change. The Council voted it down five to zero. It appeared that Galvin grew up somewhat and recognized that the word "Green" actually referred to the local environment.

The only way to explain the insanity of this proposed project is to compare it to the story of the Emperor's New Clothes. In that story everyone lives with the fantasy that the Emperor was actually wearing clothes. With the Layman street zoning application everyone was living with the fantasy of the possibility of a commercial building going up on a small vacant lot. No one said anything about the fact that project was nothing more that the developer's imagination.

In a way this event may be opening up a new direction in Charlottesville neighborhood planning. One major problem in the town was that the developers always got what they wanted. If they wanted to build a hideous building or project in the wrong section of the city they got the right to do so. The mayor and the majority of the council trusted their decision making. For a long time a number of residents have been complaining that the developers are too powerful and need to be controlled.

I told Bob and other members of the council that developers are like dogs. I am not against dogs, and love my dog. But do not let the dog run the show or the household. He is there for a purpose and he has to obey the rules and when he behaves as he is supposed to, he can do some great work. Hopefully the defeat of a well-known developer on the Lyman Street rezoning application will encourage the Council to put leashes on the developers to keep them from running wild.

We won again. But we know that there will be more fights as the neighborhood changes and as many old houses that once were converted into two or more apartments are remodeled back to being single family homes. The Council now knows that Belmont has to be taken into consideration. And the neighbors who held together for this fight were more than ever convinced that the Council was our worst enemy.

While we won most of the arguments with the Council, there was one loss on the Gumbo Palace. What is amazing to me about all of this

 STANTON BRAVERMAN

is that almost all my fights with the Council stems from only one of the houses I own in the city. They say that a man's home is his castle. The best way to describe living on Douglas Street is to say "A man's home is his fort."

With the end of the Lyman Street problem we soon found that the war was not over. In fact it came at us on three different fronts. One was the Holly Street issue. In the back of the house is what appears to be an alley and it is the access to my backyard and off street parking area which is critical to living in the house since often it is not possible use street parking because all the local businesses need it. But it is not an alley. It is shown on all the city maps as Holly Street. Along one side of the street are a number of backyards for the neighboring houses on our side of Douglas Street. But on the other side of Holly Street is a nice two or three acre size property owned by a developer that eventually will be turned into a housing project. At the present time there is only one business on Holly Street - an automotive repair shop. With almost every corner in Belmont there is a story and there is one with this lot. For years it was owned by Jimmy Ditter who was a race car mechanic and had a house and a three-bay workshop on the property. Jimmy was a "Good Old Boy" and could be tough to deal with though generally he was calm. But the word was, "Do not mess with him!" When he lived there he decided to change the name of the street to Ditter Ave. His house was set back about 600 feet from the road and he turned it into an asphalt lane that went to his front door. Since no one else used the street on a regular basis the street got to be known as Ditter Ave. Jimmy at one point got a street sign to put up that said it was Ditter Ave. Most maps refer to the street as Holly Street and other maps refer to it as Ditter Ave. Whatever the name, it is a street and not an alley.

But the developer who owns the property that was Jimmy's place would like to get rid of the street and had one of his associates call all the property owners to say that everyone agreed to petition the city to give up Holly Street and if they would like to also do so, it meant they would get 15 feet added to their backyard. This was not true. It was a lie. Not one single property owner whose property was contiguous to Holly Street likes the idea. And once again it showed that developers do not care about being truthful if it serves their purpose. But never lie to a developer because they will get upset. It is a simple immature attitude of "they can dish it out but cannot take it." As I previously stated, developers in Charlottesville seem to have the political folk in their pocket and when they want something they push very hard to get it. There is a local joke about developers and that is the only building or rezoning application that did not get approved is the one where the ink pad ran out of ink and they could not summarily stamp it "approved." And that led to the battle for Holly Street. The neighbors told the associate "No" to his proposal. To some it made no sense because on the other side of their property line is a rainwater drainage ditch that goes along most of Holly Street. As one neighbor said, "If I give up my rights to the street I will be getting a drainage ditch."

About that time Jennifer was walking Kodie, our 90 pound lab, and noticed the street sign that used to say Ditter Ave had been taken down and there was not any sign to show what street it was. This bothered her and she called the city and said that they needed to put up a sign saying it was Holly Street because in case there was an emergency the fire department and rescue squad had to know where it was. About a week later a sign was put up and it said it was Holly Street. But in the corner of the sign it had the word "private." Now everyone is paranoid at this point and they want to know why the word private is on the sign. It raised the possibility that the developer somehow got title to the street. While we got concerned about it, it was not a complicated issue. The term private refers to the fact that all the owners of the adjacent properties own it collectively and everyone has right of access. The word private is an attempt by the city not to have any responsibility for street upkeep and maintenance. It seems that around a 100 years ago a developer designed the neighborhood and put in the street. But officially the city never took over the street. It turns out that there are a lot of private streets in Charlottesville and other parts of the surrounding area. The law is clear that one adjacent property owner cannot get the city to close out this street without the agreement of all parties. It is not a problem other than we just do not trust either the city or the developers and we are still concerned that they will try to pull a fast one on us.

          STANTON BRAVERMAN

CHAPTER 22

THE JUNCTION

A T THIS POINT we are starting to calm down but thinking 'What is going on next?" And then it comes. Located in the middle of Downtown Belmont is a restaurant called the Local. Adam Frazier, when he opened it a few years ago, intended for it to be a local restaurant for the neighborhood. This was exactly what the city intended to happen when they rezoned the corner that later became known as "Downtown Belmont. We do not know if Adam really intended to keep the Local as a place for the neighborhood, but quickly it has grown into a huge complex and attracts people from all over the area. Most of the neighbors often ask how he got the city to go along with the expansion to a point that it now seats about 300 people without requiring that he find additional parking space for all the cars. The restaurant serves good food and it has become the "in" place to eat in town. The fact that there is insufficient parking for this many customers does not bother the customers. They will drive into Belmont and look for a place to park on one of the neighborhood streets. Then they get out of their cars and walk one or two or even three blocks to the restaurant. To these suburbanites who live in track houses or in huge McMansions the charm of Belmont is part of the ambiance of having dinner there. The Local has become a place where parents of the university students take their children for dinner when they come to see how they are doing. There are over 5,000 undergraduates at the University of Virginia that come from well-off families and the parents often visit to check on their children. Kodie and I often walk by the restaurant and I meet up with these families. They are nice folks who do not want loud music. Every time I walk by the Local I remember the days when my children were in college and we would go to check into what they were doing. It is an amazing happening.

There are four major costs in sending a child to a university. One is tuition, the second is room and board, third is books and study material and fourth is the cost of the dinners when you go to check on them. They greet you like buzzards that have not been fed for days. They ask if they can invite their friends along for the dinner and when they get to the restaurant, all of them immediately order the most expensive item on the menu and eat like they've never eaten before. And you, as the parent, just sit back and watch them feast on your wallet.

Even though parking is tight, people from all over the city go to the Local, as well as Mas and Tavola that are also on the corner. All of them are good restaurants. In a way, it is the charm of Belmont that attracts them. People who live in the suburbs yearn for life in the city while people who live in the city yearn for life in the countryside. No one seems to fully enjoy where they live. For the suburbanites looking for an inner city experience, Belmont is the place to visit. Many times while walking Kodie, a 90 pound Lab Husky mix, the customers who are eating on the patio of the restaurants will stare at us as if we are the lucky ones to live in that dynamic neighborhood.

With four major restaurants on one corner, surrounded by a lovely neighborhood where old forgotten houses are coming back to life, Belmont is a collage of inner city life. It is no longer an area for neighborhood convenience but rather a tourist attraction. It is not difficult to understand why it has happened. The old architecture of the buildings and houses cannot be found in many places in the New South where almost everything is newly constructed. People like to see old time living, they like the feel of a comfortable and friendly neighborhood where people sit on their porches and greet friends as they walk by on hot summer nights. It is the type of neighborhood that is rather rare in today's world and people enjoy coming here and being part of it.

I must also mention that there are two other restaurants at that spot. One is the Belmont BBQ and the other is La Taza. Both are nice places to go but I stay away from La Taza because of its history of supporting

STANTON BRAVERMAN

Bel Rio and because they tried to operate their own music venue which drove a lot of us crazy. The BBQ place is good but I am allergic to BBQ and stay away from it. But it is one more business that stares at you when you are there. Kodie loves this place. We do not put a leash on him most of the time. He knows to stay out of the streets and to stay close to me. He keeps this composure when walking around the area except when we get close to the BBQ place. He will then break ranks and go up to the front door and bark to let them know inside that "Kodie is here." Most of the time, the manager or the owner will come out and give him a morsel of BBQ – usually when a number of customers to the restaurants are walking by.

Then there is Jeff's place, the old garage that has a sign on it now that says Welcome to Downtown Belmont, Fitzgerald' Cooper Tires. It is not very big and at night there are always eight to ten cars parked on the lot.

It is fun trying to guess where the people are from. They come from all over the country and most of them enjoy their time in Belmont. One time I guessed the lady was from New Jersey or New York. It was more than her accent that said where she was from. As she walked out of one of the restaurants she looked at Jeff's tire place and loudly said to her husband, "Sammy, look at that gas station. I can see it now: a multi story condo right there. It would be perfect."

One good looking woman customer who had a nice expensive sports car parked in front of our house was getting into it and I complimented her on the nice car. "Thank you for the comment. It is really a hard top convertible and it is such a nice evening I am going to put the top down." I could not resist saying, "Wait, and let me get my camera out. I want to take a picture of your doing it. I will then post it on my Facebook page with the comment 'attractive woman takes off her top in front of my house.'" The lady laughed but I did not take the picture.

Other times, when a car on the corner is pushing to get through the traffic, they will honk their horn like it says "Move on, will you, please," and since the rule in Charlottesville is to never honk your horn, whenever someone honks you know that they are from New Jersey. Often when with Kodie I will meet up with friends who live in the suburbs or from out of town and they will say "Hey, Stan, come on over and have a drink with us." and I do and there are a lot of questions about life in Belmont. Sometimes I will brag and say it is great, everything is in walking distance. And other times I will complain that the City Council just keeps messing up the area.

Often, at about 11:00 pm when a party at one of the restaurants has just ended and the customers are walking back to their cars, while Jennifer and I are curled up in bed for the night we will hear their conversations as they say good evening to friends and their children. There will be laughing, give one more hug, promise to get together again soon. We hear the doors closing to their car and the sound of the motor as they drive away. There is always noise if you live in the inner city. But sometimes the noise is like music. There is the noise of the people, the noise of the cars, or sometimes it is their radio, the noise of a train going through, there are church bells and, at times, police sirens. But overall, to a person who enjoys life in the inner city it is more like a symphony that often puts you to sleep.

The Local is a popular place and Adam put it all together himself. I saw him build a lot of it with his own hands. He is a big fellow, but quiet. I remember when he first bought the old building and he was doing most of the remodeling and the old brick front collapsed and it has to be rebuilt. Adam got out there with the old bricks and mortar and rebuilt the wall. In addition, Adam lived in the neighborhood with his wife and children and cared for what was going on. But he soon got into a project that was over his head and that is when the trouble began. What was a great neighbor turned out to be the neighbor from hell.

Across the street from the Local, which is two doors up the hill from our house, there is a very old antique looking brick building that was part store and part residence. It was sold to Adam by Janet Hatcher. On one side, away from Douglas Street, Janet Hatcher used to live. Her house/store was on a double lot with a very large backyard. It was a corner lot with the store front at that corner and the other side was a lovely wrap-around porch that faced her side yard where huge Ash trees shaded the neighborhood. The building was in bad shape and in need of extensive remodeling. Adam bought the place from Janet and

STANTON BRAVERMAN

soon started working on it. Adam likes to keep his cards hidden and for a long time did not tell the neighborhood what he intended to do with this building. Everyone figured it would be another restaurant in Belmont. The neighbors, already concerned about the severe shortage of parking at night, were concerned but the zoning allowed for it. As usual, Adam did the work himself. He started to dismantle the insides and then got a crew to strip off the old red paint that was covering the bricks. Removing paint from bricks is always difficult and that work went on for weeks. There would be a crew of workers sandblasting the paint and another washing it down the rain water run-off drains. It was noisy and sent a mist of red stuff all over the area. As the removal project was almost complete I was talking to a contractor who was working on a building across from our house. At one point he looked at me and said, "I do not know how that fellow is able to get away with what he is doing!" I asked what he was referring to and he replied, "That old house is covered with lead paint and there are EPA regulations on getting rid of it. One thing you do not do is wash it into the rain water system because if could be drinking water for someone down the river."

That put me on notice that Adam was not so innocent and could be a serious problem. It was not clear at that time if Adam knew what he was doing or he was an amateur contractor who was making mistakes as he redid the building. When I asked him about it he replied "I am learning as I go." and I naively figured he just did not realize that the paint had lead in it. It was something to be concerned about but felt that it was too late to complain and if it was a bad experience in the learning process then he would get better at what he wanted to do.

Then about two months later the local newspapers reported that Adam had worked out an arrangement with the Chef at a very upscale restaurant in the area to take over the new restaurant that would be serving gourmet Mexican style dishes. That was the first news the neighborhood got about what he intended to do with the new building.

The conversion of the old building to a new restaurant continued. There was a lot of activity with bulldozers and debris. As part of this project Adam planned to turn the yard into a parking area for customers. To the neighbors who watched Adam try turning the yard into a parking area it seemed chaotic. He built a cinder block wall along the edge of the property to be a retaining wall and then started to fill in the area to level it off.

One day Adam asked to speak with me about the rain water runoff system of the parking lot. He said that he needed my help in establishing a way to have the excess rain water run into the drainage ditch that ran along Holly Street in the back of my house. He told me that if he could run a ten inch drainage pipe underground along the edge of my property it would solve the problem. He wanted to know if he could get an easement to build the pipe. The same request was made to Janet Hatcher who still owned the house that Shirley Shotwell lived in. We both agreed to meet for lunch at the Local to discuss it. What Janet and I did not know is that the new EPA regulations did not allow for such a rainwater runoff system and Janet and I did not see any reason to deny Adam his easement.

The lunch was fantastic, and he served Janet and me a couple of glasses of nice wine. It was a delightful lunch. The food was a lot better than anything I had ever eaten at that restaurant in the past. We were the guests of honor; the chef came out to tell us that we were sampling the cuisine that was going to be on the menu for the new restaurant. Adam was joyful and talkative. While the meal was enjoyable a message was going through my brain saying, "Watch out, there may be some first class bull shit being thrown at us". This message was caused by the wine that was served. After 40 years of legal experience I know that often, when a scam is in the works, there are alcoholic beverages at the table. And then it came. Adam gave us a document to sign that was titled "easement". He requested that we sign it and he would record it with the city. I read through it and quickly realized it was at best a very amateur document and clearly did not conform to an easement as I know it. I told Adam that I would have to get the approval of a real estate attorney Janet and I would retain to review it. Janet promptly agreed with me and we soon ended lunch. Even before I showed it to Rick Carter, the leading real estate attorney in town, I knew there would be serious problems for me and Janet if we signed it. As I read the document, it extended to Adam an undefined easement on our properties. Once we

    STANTON BRAVERMAN

signed it he could do anything with the properties he wanted to do. My experience with easements is that they are very specific and they come with detailed drawing of what it is for and should only apply to the ten feet of property along Holly Street. A couple days later at Rick Carter's office, he agreed with me and said it had to be done right. I then asked Rick if he knew the attorney who prepared the document and he said he did and the attorney did better work than the document that was given to us to sign. The fact that Adam's attorney knew better than to ask us to sign an incomplete document suggested that Adam had some sinister scheme in mind. At a minimum it would have allowed Adam to use our nice backyards as additional parking areas for his customers.

Once the new restaurant opened, Downtown Belmont would have six restaurants – Mas, the Local, Tavola, La Taza, Belmont **BBQ** and Adam's new restaurant. There is seating for about 500 people in all of them and the only parking for customers would be Adam's new parking lot that would handle 19 cars. Most of the customers parked on the adjacent streets and walked two or three blocks to get to any one of them. Already the local residents were starting to fight back over the invasion of people going to the restaurants and it was only a matter of time before it turned into a political issue. Janet and I, after realizing that Adam probably was trying to scam us, felt that he was making a stab at getting additional parking for almost no cost. I do not know why Adam thought he could get away with this scheme. I am an attorney and qualified to handle many legal issues. The only thing I assume is that he saw me as an immigration attorney who, as previously stated, are not perceived as first class members of the bar. The attorneys for the Water Authority saw me this way and were certain that I could not handle myself in court. Maybe Adam thought the same way. But it was clearly a mistake on his part that cost him a lot of money.

I went back to Adam and told him that the easement had to be specific and that detailed drawing done by a surveyor was required. He said he would correct it. Then a few days later he gave us another document to sign that said it was for a rainwater runoff system and it was for a 20 feet easement and again it was not clearly defined as to what it was for and where it would be. and no survey drawing was attached. I quickly objected because a rainwater run off system could be nothing more than bringing in a backhoe and extending the drainage ditch across my property and Janet's to his property. At this point both Janet and I said we would no longer consider the easement and that he had to find another way to get the rainwater to the ditch. When I asked Adam what on earth he or his lawyer was thinking he shrugged his shoulders and said, "It was a mistake. I got another idea on how to handle the problem." At that point I gave up on Adam because it smelled too much like the Ragged Mountain nonsense that the lawyers would hide behind when it looked like they were getting caught doing some strange stuff. The lawyer of the water authority said, "I only want to do what I did 21 times before," which I interpreted as, "It is time to run to my safety position." With Adam, if I signed the document as he requested, I could easily turn my back yard into an extension of his parking area. When I complained that the document he gave us to sign did not deal with the problem and that it gave him too much control over our property, he announced it was a big mistake. I then thought back to the lead paint issue and realized his comment "I am learning as I go" was the position he could run to if serious EPA charges were brought against him.

What we did not know at that time was that new EPA regulations for parking lots are not what they were ten years ago. There are serious environmental issues that now have to be faced. Today the lot has to deal with the proper handling of rainwater runoff that can no longer be channeled to the nearest drainage ditch and sent off to a local river. The lot has to be designed to maximize the amount of rain water that will percolate back into the ground. In the old days the yard would have been leveled off and then asphalt poured on top of it, which is what we thought Adam intended to do. Today asphalt is not used and there has to be a serious study of the soil to determine how much it can hold and how much can be percolated into the subsoil. The drainage system is only for heavy rainfalls which will saturate the soil to the point it cannot absorb more of it. Groundwater replenishment is a serious issue in the country and many cities are investing in infrastructure to assure that construction projects allow for water to be percolate underground.

     STANTON BRAVERMAN

These requirements have significantly raised the cost of construction and Adam should have been aware of these requirements. But he seemed to ignore some of them. From my position as a sidewalk superintendent it seemed that Adam just was not sure what he was going to do.

Then Adam told me that he found another way to deal with the rainwater issue. It turns out that there is a 36-inch rainwater runoff pipe that goes to the drainage ditch that runs under his property and all he had to do is to tap into it. He did not need the easement for the parking area and it looked to me as if he was just trying to scam us out our property. This just got me upset. Adam had apparently illegally disposed of a huge amount of lead paint and tried to trick us out of the use of our backyards. It was time to fight back.

The following Sunday I walked through the construction site with a friend who, who worked with me on the Ragged Mountain case. The work yard was open to everyone to walk into. It was a mess without any barriers to keep people out; there was debris scattered here and there. There was not even a rolloff to throw construction trash into. (This was a violation of construction safety practices.) My friend immediately saw major issues with the groundwater runoff and saw the massive amount of demolition and remodeling that had already been done and did not understand why the city allowed such a project to go on. She then sat down at my computer desk, went through the permits section of the city internet site and noted that there appeared to be no permits or inspection for any of the work. She then filed a request to the Building Inspector's office to review any plans Adam submitted for the property and then sent an email to the Inspector stating that in her opinion there were some serious safety issues with the construction site and it was not clear how Adam was going to deal with the runoff. I followed up with an email to the City Building Inspector listing a significant number of building code and construction code violations that we felt existed.. Within a couple of days the city issued a stop work order for any further activity on the property. It appeared that Adam was trying to build the restaurant without any permits and it was not clear as to why he thought he could get away with it. But some of the neighbors who worked for the city told me that it was easy to get the inspector's office to look the other way. I did not know what was going on but I had to do something to stop it. The email I sent to the building inspector's office met this need. Once the Inspector formally knew about the construction project and the failure to get permits he had to do look into it. If he failed to do so and the building was unsafe and people got hurt he would be responsible. I know of one project in Northern Virginia where the inspectors failed in their job, the building collapsed and the inspectors went to jail.

About a week later my friend and I went to the Inspector's office to review plans that Adam has just submitted. By this time, he had torn out all of the inside of the old building, built a second porch, did a lot of remodeling inside, put up extensive copper work on the front, built the bar and a lot of other improvements. And now he is finally getting around to asking for a permit. What we saw at the building inspectors' office was not only the drawings for a parking lot and a restaurant but two other buildings to be used for a catering operation. But the project had not yet been approved.

About a week later we were advised that Adam submitted a new set of plans and listed himself as the general contractor for the project. I passed this on to Janet who emailed me to say that at the time she sold the building to Adam they talked about not only a lead paint issue, but the probability that there was a considerable amount of asbestos in the floors of the old house. It appears that Adam holds a general contractor license. With these credentials he could not possibly hide behind "I did not know" or "I am learning as I go" statements to deal with serious building violations..

Reviewing what Adam had done with the Local, which was supposed to be a quiet neighborhood pub-like restaurant and seeing it slowly expand into a huge restaurant seating about three times the number of people that was originally planned, all of this done very quietly and without any provision for additional parking spaces for customers, I wonder how he got away with it. Some of the expansion we can figure out. The original restaurant had a very small kitchen and once opened and it became a popular place in town and there was a need to expand the kitchen. Adam submitted an application to expand it to

STANTON BRAVERMAN

about three times the size and no one cared. But what they did not tell us is that the design he submitted to the city government was to have a roof that could withstand pressure of 150 pounds per square inch. That allowed for the Local to add a full deck over the kitchen which was soon done. The neighborhood was only told about the kitchen expansion and not about the patio rooftop that would seat another hundred customers. I clearly remember the building inspector asking me if I had any objections to the enlargement of the kitchen. I said there was no objection because the old kitchen was too small and had to be expanded. It was a safety issue. What the Inspector should have asked me is if we objected to a new kitchen and rooftop patio. He had to know about the patios because the designs for the expansion called for a rooftop that could hold up a skyscraper. Then after the patio was opened Adam soon put a roof over it and then put shutters on the sides which allows for him to fully close it in at any time. And then, somehow, another deck was added and it also was enclosed. In effect he tripled the size of the business and with each expansion there was no corresponding increase in parking space for customers. On a busy Saturday night there would be about 300 customers eating dinner which implies about 100 cars that are parked throughout the neighborhood. In addition there are about 25 staff members working at that time, most of whom drove to work and also parked cars in the neighborhood. What is amazing is that the city requires one parking space at a minimum for every 500 feet of expansion. All Adam provided was one space in the back that is not accessible to any customer. While there are a number of lots for off-street parking, none of them are available for visitors to downtown Belmont. Recently in an attempt to deal with the parking issue that started on Friday and Saturday nights, Adam set up valet parking for $8. But I just do not know where they are taking these cars. Maybe he was planning on parking them in my backyard?

Thinking back at these events I remember one day the fire inspector closed down the rooftop patio because no automatic sprinklers had been installed. This led us to believe that Adam did not have a permit to expand the size of the business because if he did the inspectors would have required the installation of this system. They were not in place, the building was a fire hazard and it was only corrected once the fire department knew of the problem. At least one section of the city government is prepared to do its job.

The Local is not the only business that is adding to the parking issue. Next door to the Local is another restaurant called Tavola. It is a very good restaurant that is owned by a local well known chef who also wanted his own neighborhood restaurant. The restaurant was limited in space to the existing structure and he did not expand it and technically does not need to provide any parking space. But this restaurant is often busier than the Local since the food is fantastic. Often there will be long lines of people outside the restaurant trying to get a table. Many of them will give up waiting and go into the Local or Mas for dinner. But this restaurant brings in about 100 customers at a time which means fifty more cars parked in the neighborhood. Any person who deals with neighborhood planning can easily see that the parking situation will create serious tension between the residential houses that surround the corner. But to the City government, it is located in Belmont and the only significant improvement they made to the area is to put out a couple of recycled flower pots.

Adam starts off telling us he is learning as he goes. And while doing it he probably threw lead paint all over the neighborhood and his employees and may have improperly disposed of asbestos – both of which can be serious environmental issues. Then once, about the time he gets a stop work order, he submits an application for the permits and announces he is a general contractor. It looks to be absurd. To get certified with a class A general contractor's license a person is held responsible for EPA regulation. It is not a time to claim that "I am learning as I go" excuse. But then again there are a lot of things in Charlottesville that are absurd.

The whole project was nuts. Adam was clearly not qualified to be a general contractor. Things were chaotic. At one point he would dig up the parking area and haul a lot of dirt out only to bring it back in at a later date. He built a retaining wall to fill the lot with dirt to level it off, only to learn that the cement blocks he uses would not work. He then built a solid concrete wall that was adjacent to the block wall. One day,

STANTON BRAVERMAN

when he was working on the inside of the building he dug holes along the back wall that were six feet deep. This was being done because they just discovered that there were no footers underneath that wall and the concrete was poured to give needed support to the foundation. This is something that should have been done prior to any inside work. We saw workmen walk off the job saying that the job was a mess and they could not take it any longer. One worker told me that he would do the same work two or three times because Adam constantly changed his mind about what he wanted. A lot of this strange activity was the result of his failure to get permits. Once the inspectors got concerned about the project they required that serious engineering studies be made of the building and the project call for full compliance with building codes and EPA requirements.

All of a sudden the work on the parking area stopped. The area was redesigned to conform to EPA regulations. The retaining wall that he built did not meet code; another wall that was made of solid concrete and was higher was installed adjacent to the wall he previously built. In addition a subterranean holding tank was put in across the whole parking area that had a dirt floor and special bricks were placed above the tank to allow rain water to run off into it and to slowly percolate into the ground. The plans called for replacing the terra cotta 36 inch underground pipes that were put in 100 years ago which were part of the neighborhood runoff system.

In addition to this mess, a careful review of the construction site showed a number of dangerous issues. One was the fact that the construction site was open for anyone to walk through. Second, there was a concern that the new balcony that he added did not meet code. The brick pilings it sat on were built a century or more ago and were not strong enough to hold up the lower and the upper balcony. To strengthen them he pointed them up with concrete but the inside mortar was still weak. There was construction waste all over the yard and he never brought in one rolloff to throw the waste into. Instead he took it out in small truck loads which took forever to do. Often the trash would blow into Shirley's back yard. He also started to store supplies in the basement of the building. These supplies were for the catering operation and for the Local. This meant that a number of the employees at the Local were constantly walking across a chaotic construction site to get dishes and other supplies. These employees did not wear hard hats when on the site and they were doing it during the day when construction workers were busy and at night without proper lighting. Overall the project looked like a disaster that could happen at any time. A number of people in Belmont were asking how he could get away with such behavior without a permit. There were the usual comments that it is the "Good Old Boy" system at work. Maybe that was true or maybe Adam just was hoping to get away with it. Overall it was a mess and I was upset because I felt that his request for an easement was just a scheme to grab my backyard for additional parking space. And after building two houses and remodeling five or six of them I knew about building codes and the responsibilities of the local building inspector. My email to the inspector was to make him aware of what was going on. Once he is aware of the problem he has to promptly deal with it. That is what led to the stop work order and design modifications that cost Adam a huge amount of money and time.

After the stop work order and after Adam submitted plans for the project that were approved he started back on building the property. The focus now was the parking lot. An engineer was hired to supervise the work to assure that it was done properly; a five foot tall cinder block wall that ran about 80 feet along Janet's rental house was not up to code which led to building up against it an 8 inch concrete reinforced wall. All of the dirt he took out brought the level of the lot down too far and he had to bring in a lot of more dirt to raise it to the proper level.

There was another issue I pointed out to the Inspector and that was the health of the young men from the neighborhood who worked on the paint removal. Lead poisoning can be very serious. It not only affects a person's physical health but also his mental health. Studies have shown that one of the reasons for aggressive behavior by teenagers living in ghetto neighborhoods is because of the lead they absorb into their bodies while living in dilapidated old homes which contain massive amounts of lead paint. There were five or six young African American men from the neighborhood who did the work. It was clear that they were not trained for dealing with lead paint. They all did what Adam told them to do and that was to blast it off and then wash it down the street drain with the hose. Once the job was over, they were gone; with the neighborhood changing as it had been, they seemed to move out.

But the inspector's office reply did not mention that he followed up on this health hazard. He assured me that in the future the project will be done as required by the building code. This is a shocking situation. Here we have five or so young men who may now have massive amounts of lead poisoning and the inspector's office just is not concerned. The healthcare that they are likely to need sometime in the future will be paid by them or Medicaid, and that assumes they actually get any medical treatment.

CHAPTER 23

RAMBLING ON

IF ADAM DID this in Canada or any western developed country with a single payer healthcare provider he would have gone to jail. In Canada there are safety inspectors in every town and village who go around and observe construction sites. If they see a man on a roof without a safety harness they will cite that person for a violation and the employer will face a complicated safety review and fine. The Province has a simple reason for being so difficult and that is because the Province will pay the bill for anyone who is hurt in an accident. The safety inspector is there to keep people safe and it is part of their healthcare system that keeps people healthier than in the United States at about half the cost per person.

This situation of the lead paint being thrown all over the neighborhood just eats at me. The more I think about it the more bothered I get. Friends often tell me to "back off" since I am 73 years old, to go fishing and enjoy life. But in the United States, things seem so out of balance I find it difficult to just push it aside to go fishing. One thing that I have learned over the years is how interrelated everything is to everything. The cavalier attitude that Adam showed in blowing the lead all over the place is indicative of the overall lack of respect and understanding that is often held by the business community. There is a need for health reform and a need to control the business community instead of them controlling us.

In Canada there is a lot of pressure from the government to keep healthcare costs down. In the US, the system works the other way. The State governments do not know how to keep costs down because the lobbyists from the business community keep pressuring the government to ignore the long term costs and to focus on just the immediate cost to the employer. They are walking the halls of our legislatures telling the legislators things like, "If you impose stricter and enforceable safety standards, then companies will not be able to hire many people and that will tend to increase the unemployment level." The legislators then take the money from lobbyists and then tell everyone that we need to keep short term costs down and when it comes to the longer term costs, the same lobbyists tell us not to worry about it until it happens. It could be years away; by then it will be a problem for other politicians.

When it comes to healthcare in the US, there is a mistrust of government and the feeling is to leave healthcare to the private sector. But the private sector has messed up healthcare far more than the government would have done if they had taken over the health insurance business and established a single payer insurance program. Had the government set up a single payer health insurance company then Adam would never have gotten away with what he did. But instead the US has a chaotic situation. The public does not trust the government and they are slowly learning not to trust private-run healthcare organizations. Many people say that the real problem is the influence of the lobbyists that have been sanctified by the Supreme Court in the Citizens United case. To control them would interfere with the constitutional right to free speech and that corporations are to be treated as people and all constitutional rights are vested in them. But corporations owe their existence to the state governments who issue corporate charters for them to perform a specific function. On the one hand they insist that they need to operate without government interference and on the other hand they go to the government to give them the documents that allow for them to exist. If the government has the right to mandate their methods of operation then surely the government has the right to limit their activity. Earlier in this book the reader read about RWSA and how its charter allowed for them to sell bonds but limited the collateral to only revenue. There is clearly a public purpose for this limitation. I would not be surprised that with the next bond that RWSA sells it will once again include all sorts of items for collateral even though the banks do not require it. They may even argue that the Supreme Court in the Citizens United decision gave them the authority to overlook any restriction on their behavior. They may argue that they have a constitutional right to engage in free enterprise in the US now that they have been created. But the argument makes no sense. The United States is a country that believes that humans were created by God. It conforms to the language of the Constitution. "We hold all men to be created equal by our creator" is the language in the preamble and then the constitution goes on to limit what men can do. Then once a state under the authority of the Constitution creates a corporation, it is then treated as if it is a human and they get the right to "Life, liberty and the pursuit of happiness" which Corporate America interprets as meaning "They can do as the damn well please."

At the present time Corporate America has become so brazen that they often just ignore any limitations imposed on them; in part this is because they believe that nobody is out there to stop them and second, they have the money to hire lobbyists to get the legislature to change the law so that what they want to do goes from being illegal to legal. While preparing for the Ragged Mountain case I did some inquiry into the Nestle Foundation and could not understand how the purpose of the non-profit tax exempt organization related to their support of the Moorman River. Maybe it is there someplace, but it was not readily available and maybe it is just another example of corporate (this case a non-profit corporation) doing whatever they want to do. Nonprofits have to file for a special exemption from the Internal Revenue Service to operate as a tax exempt organization. They have to state a specific social purpose they are trying to achieve. If they wander away from that goal then they can lose their tax exempt status. Nestle, like many companies, has set up tax exempt foundations and charities to meet public needs usually related to their general business operations. For example, a drug company may set up a non-profit organization to distribute their drugs to families living at the poverty level. There is a clear nexus between them. But apparently not with Nestle, who is in the business of bottling water, and I just do not understand how that relates to "Saving the Moorman River".

As the American public gets more and more concerned about corporate abuse of power they may once again turn to government

     STANTON BRAVERMAN

agencies to take over some of the activities that are being poorly done by the private sector. The real problem is the lobbyists and their money. But the interference by the lobbyists in the government is similar to the interference by developers in the local city government. Not only are developers to be treated like dogs, but the same treatment should be extended to the lobbyist. They cannot run the government; they cannot have the final voice because their self-interests often run against the interests of real humans. Corporations, if they are to be treated as if they are human. then have to act like they are mature humans with compassion for their fellow man, concern about society and willingness to be a positive force in our lives. To the extent that they refuse to be mature then "We the people" have the right to remove them from the political arena. Yet Adam is incorporated in various ways and it looks as if he feels it gives him the same right as Nestle, which is to do what they want, where they want to do it and nobody is supposed to get in their way. It is not an issue of the government taking over our lives but rather it is the business community (that is businesses large and small) that have taken over government and through the power of the government they are taking over our lives.

The issue with Adam is not over. Maybe the Inspector's office will straighten things out or maybe Adam will still do as he wants. Maybe someone in the city government will notify the public health department or the Environmental Protection Agency of the lead issue and they will follow up. Or maybe Adam, who is now part of the business community, has the God-given right to do as he sees fit.

CHAPTER 24

WHO OWNS THE DRAINAGE PIPE?

THE WAR WITH the City Council is not over. There are other horrors created by the city government. It turns out that there is a serious question as to who owns the rainwater runoff pipe that we recently discovered also goes across my property. You cannot find a recorded easement in the city records that refers to the pipe. It takes rain water from blocks around that flows into street drains and then under Adam's place, Janet's rental house and my yard and then into a ditch that runs through the woods and on to someplace. Under current EPA regulations, this system is a vital part of the city environment. I only recently learned about the pipe being there. The problem is that no one claims ownership or responsibility for maintaining it even though the city raised everyone's real estate taxes to raise funds to meet the new EPA requirements. It looks like they got the money and apparently are going to spend it someplace else. At a meeting with an official of the city government I was told that maintenance of the pipe was my responsibility. That is insane. Imagine if the electric company told homeowners that they are responsible for maintaining the outside telephone pole and line. The pipe serves a number of neighbors who have no responsibility to maintain it and the city looks to me, who gets no utility out of it to keep it in good shape. They must be nuts. The City Government says that they have a constructive easement (that has never been recorded in the land records) that developed over time which allows for them to continue using the pipe. But with every easement comes a responsibility to maintain that easement. The electric company hires work crews to keep open the power lines. They do not say that the homeowner has this responsibility. If they fail to maintain it then it is technically and legally abandoned property and I should have the right to do as I want with it. This issue will not be resolved until I go to court on it which may be soon.

CHAPTER 25

WHY ME?

OVER THE YEARS I have lived in Philadelphia, Pennsylvania; Alexandria, Virginia; Rockville, Maryland; Washington, DC; St. Michaels, Maryland; Arlington, Madison County and Charlottesville Virginia. I lived in all of them, except Charlottesville, as a quiet citizen with little involvement with the local government. Some of the local governments were well-run and others were not very well-run, but they all meet minimal standards. And then when I got to Charlottesville and started living on Douglas Ave, things went crazy. There was one fight after another. There was never an end to it. The neighbors know that there will be more battles to be fought. And the question is "What is going on?" A lot of people have their views on what is happening. But it is difficult to make sense out of this chaos. One definition of chaos is that it is a complicated system that has an order that human beings cannot grasp because there are limits in our ability in using our intelligence. We often explain chaos by saying. "There is a method to the madness." When that happens we resort to theories as to why events take place. No one ever gets it right but at times it may appear to be the right way to deal with the problem.

At first I thought that Charlottesville was going through the same phase that Arlington County did in the 1970s. Back then, it was a small suburb of Washington DC. It was sealed off from Washington because there were not a sufficient number of bridges that crossed the Potomac River. The local government was run along the lines of the "Good Old Boy" system that permeates small towns in Central Virginia. Everyone knew each other and there was a general caring for the town and the people and accommodations were made for everyone with few people being left out. There often was not any need to comply with legal requirements because everyone benefited from the way things were done and by taking care of each other. Outsiders were welcome but not considered to be an important part of the community and if they stayed around it was OK to cheat them with the hope they will eventually leave. Most of the outsiders had come from Northern states where social and moral behaviors were different. My brother in law, who was raised in Weston, Massachusetts and moved to Houston, which in the early 1980s was another southern town, told me that on TV the sheriff announced that Yankees who moved into the area were like hemorrhoids in that they hurt real bad when they were around and when they leave they were no longer a pain in the "you know where". This statement could have applied years ago to Arlington.

But over time and after a few bridges were built to alleviate the congestion in crossing the Potomac, more Yankees moved into the area and slowly they influenced the local politics. Today, in Central Virginia, when you mention Alexandria, Arlington and Fairfax counties they are viewed as part of Yankee territory, yet over time Arlington matured into one of the best-run counties in the country. If this analogy is correct then all I have to do is to wait until more Yankees come into the city and this will change. To me, the problem with the noise of Bel Rio was the dying voice of a political system that would soon be gone.

If we go back to the 1960's and look at what was happening in the Washington DC metropolitan area you will observe some interesting trends. After World War II the city began a huge growth spurt and people were rapidly moving into the area. There was a need for more homes which led the developers to plan huge suburban communities that were located around the city. In Fairfax County, Virginia and Montgomery County, Maryland the developers built one community after another. At that time energy prices were still low which allowed for the new residents to use a lot of gas to get to work and the houses were so poorly built that many did not have any insulation. There were communities where the developers, or dogs as I often refer to them, were in charge and by the end of the 1970s both countries were consider two clear examples of the worst of urban planning in America and when the first energy crisis hit the country in 1972 they were in trouble. There were long lines at gas stations for gas; people were getting angry. I avoided the problem by moving to Swann Street. The energy crisis was solved for me by walking to work. But it took three years for the folks who lived out in the county to realize that inner city life was a nice way to live. Once they started looking into inner city property the developers showed up on Swann Street and the neighborhood looking for projects. Suburbanites are a strange mixture of people. When I first moved to Swann Street they told me I was crazy and that I would get killed living on that street. Three years later, when the house I bought for $30,000 was worth about $80,000, they were again telling me I was crazy, but this time it was because I did not buy every house on the block.

Life on Swann Street was so much more refreshing than the suburbs. My sons came down on weekends by bus and we would walk all over the city and visit museums and art galleries; they helped work on the house as new wiring and plumbing were put in. They quickly met all of the local African American kids on the block and they would be hanging out on the front stoops of the houses. The neighbors were great and caring. Many of them were grandmothers who were taking care of their grandchildren. My two favorite characters on the street were Mrs. Taylor and William Thomas, our neighbor. Mrs. Taylor was about 85 years old and sat on her stoop on nice days and whenever I walked by her house I had to stop and talk with her. She lived with other old relatives in a run-down house that needed repairs. Often on Sunday morning when I would be sitting on the stoop reading the newspaper she would come up to me wearing her best dress, a big fancy hat with netting and her fox head scarf, things that were fashionable in the 1930s

"Mr. Stan, could I borrow five dollars from you to take a taxi to church?"

"Mrs. Taylor, you know I am not going to lend you five dollars; I will do better. I will drive you to church." She would then get in my old VW beetle and I would roll down the windows. As we drove through the streets of the inner city to the church which was three blocks away I would be singing one of the few spirituals that I knew. There was Stan Braverman, wearing a white tee shirt driving an 85 year old Black neighbor who was all dressed up in a way that some Black folk love to

          STANTON BRAVERMAN

look like when they are at church and I would be singing, "Swing Low, Sweet Chariot, Coming For to Carry Me Home" as loud as I could.

There was so much humanity on that street I soon realized how boring life in the suburbs could be. On the corner of Swann and 15th street was a storefront church that had services on Sunday and many times I could hear the congregation singing their gospel songs and saying their prayers. They would be singing great music and clapping their hands and some were stamping their feet and it all focused on how happy they were with life. Hearing this music at times I would remember the words to the opera Porgy and Bess: "I got plenty of nothing and nothing is plenty for me. I got my heart, I got my soul, I got my misery. The folks with plenty of plenty got a lock on their doors. They are hoping no one is going to rob them while they are out there making more. What the hell, I am glad I'm alive."

And that was exactly how I felt as I heard that church service. William Thomas or Thomas was an African American who had a nice job working for the city building inspectors' office and his wife, if I remember right, also worked for the city. Thomas was educated and easily could have slipped into a middle class neighborhood in the suburbs. But he decided to make Swann Street his home. He completely remodeled his house, which was next door to my house. It was done before I got there. To Thomas there was no other place to live. It was not a question of going back or staying with the Black community but rather the same desire I had of living in the inner city. His house was so nice that once the street got known by the developers and real estate agents they would ask Thomas to allow them to show his house during a walking tour of the neighborhood. They never asked for my house to be on the tour. Though they did ask for me on a Sunday to put up a ladder on the side and pretend I was working on the house, which I agreed to do. They wanted the presence of a White Man while they were showing a house that they recently renovated.

Thomas would often tell me "Get that dog of yours off my stoop." and I would call Poochie over to our stoop. I never knew if Thomas disliked the dog or if he was just razzing me. Poochie was another of the neighborhood characters. He was mostly Border Collie which I soon learned are one of the smartest dogs. One day I took my two sons to the local McDonald's which was located at about 17th and R Streets, next to a liquor store and across from a Safeway supermarket. Poochie was a stray dog that survived by eating thrown-away foods from McDonald's customers. The next door liquor store was a hangout spot for a number of men in the neighborhood who often would have a beer or some other drink hidden in their jackets. Some of them would be drunk and when they were, would kick the dog out of their way. When we found him and realized he was no one's dog we put a leash on him and took him home. We had him for a day when Mrs. Bowie knocked on our door demanding to know what we did with her dog. She was as old as Mrs. Taylor and when we opened the door we could see she had another dog on a leash. She said Poochie was her dog because at times she would stop by the store and feed him and she wanted to know what we were doing with him. Jennifer invited her into the house and made a cup of coffee for her and they talked about a lot of things that were going on in the neighborhood. After we told her we were good friends with Mrs. Taylor who she knew she said, "Well, I will give him to you if you take care of him." which we agreed to do and thanked her for the dog. Then she announced that she would have to come by to visit us to see if we were responsible dog owners which we said we would agree to. So Poochie got a home, Mrs. Bowie got the right to come by for a cup of coffee and we got one of the smartest dogs I ever saw and Thomas got the right to tell me to get that dog off of his stoop. It seemed that Poochie liked Thomas and whenever Thomas came out of his house to sit on the stoop, the dog would sit down next to him.

There was one problem with Poochie. Often when Black men would walk down the street, he would go after them and send them running. At first I thought he had a problem with racial prejudice but we soon realized he only did it to Black men who had the smell of liquor on them. I still felt that the dog was racially prejudiced and I approached a number of Black neighbors to apologize. "Oh no, Stan, You let that dog be as he is. We do not want those men walking down this street any more than Poochie does."

STANTON BRAVERMAN

As I said, the dog was smart. He was a street dog and we could not keep him in the house when we went to work. He wanted to be left outside, in the inner city. He would travel through the neighborhood, sometimes visiting Mrs. Bowie. He had no problem crossing busy streets. Poochie could climb chain link fences that were as high as six feet. I remember one day a man drove by the house when I was sitting on the stoop with the dog. He yelled out. "Is that your dog?" and I said it was mine. "Then you get the puppies." I asked for the details and he said he had a cocker spaniel that went into heat and he was planning on breeding her with a show dog. But Poochie climbed the fence and got to the female first. I never did see the puppies but if they were half as smart as our dog they would be great dogs. Poochie's greatest achievement was when we took him to the veterinarian for a checkup and shots. We left him there and about three hours later the vet called to say the dog escaped. He was upset and did not know what to do because he never heard of a dog escaping. I told Jennifer and she cried but I assured her that even though the vet was on the other side of the city, miles away from Swann Street he would find his way home. For two day Jennifer cried over the dog and then she took the VW and went up and down the streets looking for him. She found a black ball of fur on the lawn of a house on 16th street. She yelled out "Poochie" and the head of a dog shot up into the air and she was once again united with her dog.

At the time I bought the house on Douglas Street in Charlottesville, it reminded me of the early days on Swann Street. At the time Douglas was clearly the poorer end of town. Across the street from the house was a beat-up old house that has fantastic architectural history that went back more than 100 years. Living there was a happy bunch of drunks. Three doors down was an African American woman who was raising her son and grandson. Up the street, on the corner was the Belmont market, where a number of the local poor men gathered to hang out and have a beer hidden in a paper bag. A block away was a United Methodist Church that rang church bells that were heard through the neighborhood at various times during the day. The house, like the house on Swann Street, was very close to the heart of the city which was a half mile away and a few of the houses had already been restored. It was clear that what was then happening in Belmont in 2005 was exactly what happened in Washington DC in 1976. We bought the house and waited to see what would happen. We estimated it would take three years before anyone realized the value in the neighborhood and in the meantime we would enjoy the people that lived there and do what we could to improve the community.

But it did not take long. The following summer, every weekend there would be a number of U-Haul trailers on the street with some people moving out and some moving in. By the end of the summer it was a different neighborhood. Yet this change was ignored by the City Council. Major Barry, when he saw it happen in DC, supported it because the city needed our money. Charlottesville at the time was also a poor city whose government always said it needed money but it appeared not to be interested in what was going on in Belmont. At that time the developers, who actually ruled over neighborhood, and the community planning office were still focused on the suburbs. They were building houses in the suburbs as fast as they could. By then it was getting to the peak of the housing bubble and people were buying houses in the suburbs and flipping them as fast as they could. Most new housing at that time was sold to investors who had no intention of living there. They had to sell as fast as they could since the rental income they got from renting out the house was not enough to cover the mortgage payment, which to me was a strong signal that the housing boom would soon bust. Many people bought and flipped a house and then went on and did it again, taking the profits from the first sale and using them to fund the purchase of another house.

And then the housing market collapsed and many people lost their homes and their life's savings. In the suburbs there were whole developments with new houses that could not find a buyer. At the same time, housing values in the inner city stayed where they were and the few builders that made any money that year were the ones who built homes in the inner city. There the prices either held steady or increased and builders, who often lack imagination and did not go bankrupt, flocked to find inner city developments.

          STANTON BRAVERMAN

In Belmont the price of real estate continued to increase and the City Council failed to recognize Belmont as a comeback section of town; they still saw it as the poorer end and neglected it. They allowed Bel Rio to remain open and to make so much noise that it almost ruined the place; they were reluctant to stop La Taza from turning the alley into a rock music center. Later the zoning board was willing to let a developer rezone a residential section for a multi storey office complex even though no one wanted it. They were slow in catching Adam at his apparent violations of environmental violations.

CHAPTER 26

TIME TO SOLVE THE RIDDLE

NOW THE QUESTION is, why did the city council ignore this part of town? My first answer to this question is that Charlottesville is known for being haughty. The city residents see themselves as being a community of elite people. They have a great university, the University of Virginia, which also has a great basketball team. Their hospital center is allegedly known as world renowned. As a result the Council focused most of its attention on the university and the hospital. When the neighborhood where students lived needed a new bridge, they built it. When the area around the hospital needed to be repaired, it was done. When that neighborhood needed police protection they got it. As far as Belmont was concerned, well, those are the poorer folks, they really do not need that much and they are an easy bunch of people to push around. And the council still does not understand the value of the neighborhood.

I am into conspiracy theories. Friends have often told me to forget the theories but truthfully, I enjoy them and a number of them years later turn out to be true. Usually these conspiracy theories originate because of something that personally involved me. And a lot of them arose from my law practice specializing in immigration law located in Washington DC, the capital of the US and the city of lots of intrigue. Things came across my desk many times that were hard to explain and the only way I could explain it was to dream up a conspiracy. Some of the issues and problems are described in my book titled "Undocumented Truths." In that book are a number of stories. Some were true, some were not true and some are a composite of truth and fantasy. But one imagined conspiracy related to this book and the issues facing Belmont. Most people may not get the connection but I do. George Orwell in one of his short stories states that all things are related to politics. Even a discussion about tea pots from China involves politics. With that in mind here is my story.

One day I got a friendly phone call from the FBI telling me they wanted to meet with me to serve me a subpoena to a hearing before the Grand Jury at the Federal Courthouse in Alexandria. I arranged to meet them; they served me with the subpoena and they told me that I was not a target for the investigation. If a person believes that story then we may be able to sell them the Brooklyn Bridge. The subpoena related to an old case of an employee of the Saudi Embassy. In 1998 he said he had a job offer with an employer and wondered if I could use that job offer to get him a green card. It seemed like a straightforward case. The client had been working for many years with the embassy, he was from Pakistan and he was about ready to retire. He had been out of Pakistan for many years and did not want to return. He could not immigrate to Saudi Arabia since they are tight on allowing in new immigrants. I started to work on the case but soon the sponsoring employer closed down and the application died. The man said he would come back when he got another job offer.

About a year after that I had open heart surgery and was out of the office for long periods. Mike Lin, my partner took over the case and when I returned the client had another job offer, an approved alien labor certification and an interview was scheduled for the final step in getting his green card. I accompanied him to the interview, it was approved and as we returned to the office I reminded the client that he had to leave the embassy and work for the employer, which he assured me that he was prepared to do. When I got back and gave the file to Mike and said everything went OK I requested that he send to the client an email to once again impress on him the fact that he had to work for the employer. The law office had learned from other cases that employees at the embassy who have diplomatic protection would at times fail to leave the job and when that happened it would amount to fraud. One case we had was when an embassy employee was represented by another lawyer who did not impress upon the client that he had to give up his job.

The client found himself in proceedings in the Immigration Court to revoke his green card and it took years to straighten out the problem. The Pakistani client emailed Mike to say that he had been working for the employer for a while, but the green card had not come in the mail and he wanted to know how long he had to stay on the job. Mike checked with the DHS as to the status of the green card and the comment they gave us suggested that they were investigating the case. To me, this was the result of an agency investigation to determine whether or not the client was working at the job and since he said he was, then it was only a matter of time until they finished the investigation. That was in 2004 – three years after the 9-11 disaster. The investigation took a lot of time; the client got upset and said he had friends in the Embassy who could lean on the government to move the case. Soon after he told us that, the DHS issued the green card. As far as we know, they never investigated the issues or if they were investigating then they abruptly dropped it.

It is about ten years later and the client on his own filed for US citizenship and there is a question as to where he works and how long he has been working there. He states on the application that he worked at the Embassy for many years and did not show any history of employment to the sponsoring company. It looks like someone had given him legal advice because he was well past the statute of limitation for fraud on the government and it looked like the government could no longer bother him. But there was another problem. The naturalization form also asks if the applicant had ever committed a crime for which he had never been arrested. It is a bullshit question that only a government employee could dream up, but it bit my old client because he said no to the question and the government said he lied because the way he got the green card was by fraud which is a crime and he had never been prosecuted for it. This lie was the reason for the grand jury investigation. But there was every indication that the government was after something else which was a lot more serious. They wanted to know what happened in the Saudi Embassy at the time of the attack on the World Trade Center and the Pentagon. There were a number of rumors in Washington that

     STANTON BRAVERMAN

the Saudi Ambassador had more knowledge of the terrorist attack than the embassy was admitting to and the government agents wanted my client to tell them about what he saw and knew. It was well known in Washington that the Bush administration was very close to the King of Saudi Arabia and as long as they were in office they could not find Osama Bin Laden. He was only found and killed by the Obama administration, which was not close to the monarchy. My client apparently got the embassy to lean on the government to approve his green card even though there was an investigation going. But, when he filed for naturalization it was under the Obama administration and they reopened the investigation. It was amazing. Here is this dinky issue that does not amount to anything being a focus of a grand jury investigation. When I got the subpoena, I refused to cooperate at first since I had to adhere to attorney client confidentiality standards; the government then presented the issue to the Federal District Court in Alexandria to waive the attorney client confidentiality which meant I had to testify against my client. It was necessary for me to hire an attorney who insisted that we have an immunity agreement with the government in case somehow or other they claimed I was a party to the fraud. As I said before, even though the FBI told me that I was not a suspect in a crime, no one should accept that statement as having any value because they can quickly change their minds.

A couple of days before the hearing when I was scheduled to testify we met with the US Attorney in his conference room. There were a number of people at the table who were government attorneys, FBI agents and officers from other agencies. They asked a lot of questions about what I remembered about a case that was closed out over ten years prior to the meeting. Since I was retired and no longer had control over any files, I could not provide them with any documents that they requested. There was not much about the case that I remembered and I honestly and truthfully answered their question. It was an interesting meeting because as they asked me questions I got a better understanding as to the reason for the Grand Jury investigation. They told of strong evidence that the client not only did not work for the employer but had the employer wrote a payroll checks to him and after each check was cashed the client wrote a personal check to the employer for the exact amount of the payroll check.

When I realized what he did I was annoyed and felt that the fraud was on me as well as the government. Once they were satisfied that I was not a party to this activity, mainly because after investigating my office and not finding any malpractice in representing clients, they turned the interview into a meeting to determine the legality of the criminal proceedings and if it could lead to a removal order for the client and his family. It turned out that I understood immigration law a lot better than they did. In the end the US Attorney withdrew the subpoena.

The Grand Jury issued an indictment against my client and I later found out that the client entered into a plea agreement with the government. He pleaded guilty to a criminal charge; I do not know what it was. It may have been the charge on the indictment or they could have reduced the charges to a lower level crime. At that point I lost all contact with the client and his attorney. But then a couple of months later something strange happened. All of a sudden Saudi Arabia announced that it would no longer use its power over the oil market to control the price of crude oil. Officially they announced that there was overproduction and it got out of control. But my conspiracy mind says that the grand jury investigation and the sudden decision by Saudi Arabia are connected. My feeling is that the US Government now had collaborative evidence that the Saudis were heavily involved in planning for the terrorist attack on 9-11 and the Obama administration was now able to extract something out of them and that was to drop out of OPEC.

While this may be an interesting story to the reader the question is, what does this have to do with Belmont? To answer that question, let's go back to the words of the old professor who said that inner city development would not take place as long as energy prices are low. And his advice turned out to be correct. As the cost of energy increased over the years the inner cities throughout the country came back to life and now that the cost of energy is once again cheap, then the question is whether the trend will go the other way, back towards the development

     STANTON BRAVERMAN

of the suburban areas? It is an interesting question and important to Belmont's future development.

The way the relationship between the city and the county works is to keep Belmont and a couple of other neighborhoods in the city as holding areas for poor whites and blacks. The ccounty does not want them living in their neighborhoods. It is a hangover of the days of Jim Crow, except now it is aimed at poor people in general. In a sarcastic way integration has moved the country forward. We no longer discriminate against people because of the color of their skin but because they are poor. The Civil Rights movement has recognized that the concept of being Black is not so much an issue about the color of a person's skin but rather their lifestyle. Poor Whites and poor Blacks have integrated into one unwanted community and Belmont was to be the holding pen. The local elementary school has a much higher percentage of poor students getting free lunches than any other school in the city even though members of the Council have publicly said that this has to be corrected. Even the local real estate agents play the game by telling potential home buyers the section of the town where the better schools are located. They cannot say that the poor folks are in one area and the smart kids are in another area because that brings them to close to discussing racial issues. Instead they will tell the client that a neighborhood school has a higher achievement standard. At one City Council meeting I attended the Council mentioned that the disparity between the schools should be corrected by bussing kids from one school to another. But this was only a point for discussion and not a serious issue. It will languish as an agenda item as does the need to rebuild the Belmont bridge.

One day while thinking about this issue I remembered something Bob said while working on the addition to the house. Bob said that each year the City got $14 million from the country as a form of revenue sharing. The payment goes back to the 1980's when the city would expand as it grew and it was eating away at the county. The county did not want the city to officially grow out that far and they signed an agreement with the city to give them a large amount of money to keep from expanding. The apparent purpose of the agreement was an attempt to keep the poor whites and blacks in the city and to keep them out of the suburbs. It was about this time that Vinegar Hill was demolished and many poor black families were moved into city run subsidized housing complex. It was a blatant attempt for discrimination in housing and education. It was designed to keep poor neighborhoods as they were. There is no other reason that makes any sense. If the city absorbed a suburban neighborhood the children who lived in that neighborhood would be incorporated into the city school system and that was scary to a large number of white suburban families.

As I remembered Bob's comment and went through the city budget for 2014 there was a reference to "City County revenue sharing" and that year it was over $11 million but had been as high as $14 million. As I thought about the issue a number of things started to make sense.

When we got to Swann Street in DC, Marian Barry was glad to see us because he wanted our money. He was willing to make us feel secure while living in what was known as dangerous neighborhoods. The issue was different in Charlottesville; they did not need the money because they received this huge transfer – amounting to well over 10% of their budget requirements just for doing nothing to the neighborhood. The effect of the agreement was to keep the poor where they are and the money will continue to be paid. The money is not earmarked for a special purpose, just added to the general fund and then spent all over the city with very little spent in Belmont. It is an amazing fraud on the poor people of Belmont. The money is given to keep the poor out of the county but they do not get much of a benefit from it. If the City Council took that money each year and spent it on Belmont it would make it a highly developed section of the city.

In 1955, in the Supreme Court case of Brown v. the School Board was approved by the Court, all school districts had to integrate. It was no longer permissible to have schools for white children and others for black children. I was at Overbrook High in Philadelphia at that time and our school had always been integrated and the students just did not understand why the decision was so controversial. But in the South, the decision was a shock and there was a lot of resistance to it. There were not many people in the White community that wanted to see their schools integrated. At the time Charlottesville was a small Southern town and

　　　STANTON BRAVERMAN

they went along with the views of the rest of the South. At one point the schools in Charlottesville closed down for a couple of years. There were a number of efforts to find a back door approach to returning to integrated schools. Charlottesville and Albemarle County found a solution. A few years later another Supreme Court decision put a limit on the scope of integration. It ruled that is stopped at the end of the local school district. That meant that the city had to integrate their schools and the country has to do likewise. But the City and the county were separate units even though they were in the same metropolitan area. But if the city expanded as it had the right to do then the incorporated section would have to be integrated as determined by the city. The fear was that as the area developed the city would incorporate huge sections of the country and then there would be an influx of poor Black students. To the residents of the county this possibility had to stop. And this was done by bribing the city with a revenue sharing program. It in effect said we do not want your students in our neighborhoods and we have the money to pay you off. They effectively neutralized the decision in Brown v, School Board that each school district had to integrate. By 1980 the suburban areas around the city were becoming more and more economically integrated into a metropolitan area and the city and the county should have come together to form one local governmental organization. But the school districts where the children who lived in the new suburbs were currently going to school were primarily white middle class students. That school district had very little understanding on how to deal with the poorer kids who lived within the city limits and there was a concern that if the city expanded, their children would be going to schools that were not as good as the existing school.

About ten years ago the State Constitution was changed and the city no longer has the right to expand any further. Instead they got the right to merge with the surrounding county. In the past the city could annex parts of the county whenever they saw it to be appropriate and now they could no longer do this. The legislature in Richmond decided that it was better to have counties that acted as if they were cities. This was particularly true in areas where the metropolitan area of a city expanded well far into the surrounding county. For example Arlington

County is often referred to as the City and County of Arlington. It's the same with Alexandria. It is clearly a more efficient way to manage large metropolitan areas. It avoids the need to duplicate city services such as police department, schools etc. If the city decided to disband the county has no choice but the merge with them. And today the purpose of the revenue sharing program is to encourage the city not to disband because the county, for the same reason they did not want the city to expand its borders, just does not want to deal with a lot of poor people.

In retrospect, the move to Charlottesville was a mistake. I assumed the city wanted to greet me when I arrived because I would be paying income and property taxes in an urban area that appeared to need additional revenue. Surely, with a prominent university in the city they would understand this basic economic fact. City Councils are always looking for ways to increase tax revenue so they could improve the neighborhood, and deal with important social services and educational needs of poor families. Washington DC wanted to come back and be a vibrant place to live. And in many cities throughout the United States this has worked for the betterment of the community. But Charlottesville did not want to do that. They felt that the county was the place where new residents would want to live. Kathy Galvin, who is on the City Council expressed this clearly, when she told the audience about why she supported the Ragged Mountain project and that was the growth in the area would be in the county. She said that is where the new jobs come from and it was important that the city placate the county.

When I told the City Council that Marian Barry ran a better government I did not realize that they just did not care and that they did not want Belmont to become a comeback neighborhood. There was no financial incentive to convince the Council that Belmont could and should come back. The current system served them well; they got millions of dollars a year from the county to spend on the areas around the university and in the upper class neighborhoods and all they had to do was keep the people who lived in Belmont locked in place so they do not venture into the county. That is why the City Council could not find money to replace the Belmont Bridge, That is why they let Jim Baldi destroy the neighborhood with a hope that it would go back

 STANTON BRAVERMAN

to being as it was over the years and why they took up the nice brick crosswalk. They just did not care. They did not want to have happen in Charlottesville what was happening in many cities in the country where neglected inner city neighborhoods were being developed, where many middle class families were moving in, where many poor families found places to live in the suburbs.

And yet, what they hoped would not happen did happen. Belmont just had too much going for it. There was location, nice homes, friendly people and the price of real estate was cheap. Young families moved in because the trend in America was to live in a city and to forget the suburban areas. People were trading places; neighborhoods became integrated with rich and poor, whites and blacks living next door to each other. In Washington DC the movement took over the whole city including sections that were seen as dangerous and are now gentrified. The same happened in New York City, Philadelphia and other cities. And now it was in Charlottesville and the Council and the city government could not stop it. Not until the Council realized that it had to turn down the rezoning on Lyman Street did the Council begin to understand that abusing Belmont was not a smart move. There were a number of middle class families living there who voted in elections, who had support from friends throughout the city and the Council could no longer just say "Oh, it is Belmont, let the developers do what they want."

As a result of the revenue sharing plan, racial relations in the city are bad and are not improving. But the poor vote and they elected a Black man to the Council. The Black community came to him and asked to do something about the statue of Robert E. Lee that was in the middle of the main city park. They saw is as a message to them that the white community is still in charge. That led the Council to pass a resolution to remove the statute which in turn upset the ultra-right and led to the riots that were seen by the whole world. If the City and the County merged and became one community then the city would no longer be the holding pen for poor people and there is a good chance the riots would never have happened. But racial prejudice still predominates the area and not many people want to have the two jurisdictions merge. As a result the city is a time bomb that is slowly ticking away. One neighborhood after another is being gentrified and the poor, whites and blacks, are getting squeezed. They are not welcome in the county and there is no long a poor section in the city. They are demanding low cost housing. A few units will be built but not enough and every day the pressure goes up. If there is one more riot then Charlottesville and the surrounding area will no longer be seen as charming Southern town that is worth living and investing in.

        STANTON BRAVERMAN

CHAPTER 27

RAMBLING ON AGAIN

THEN IN 2014 an amazing thing happened. Almost overnight, when Saudi Arabia announced that it would no long support the price of oil, the price collapsed and gasoline in Charlottesville fell to under $2 a gallon. If an adjustment is made for consumer price increase and inflation over the years, the cost of gasoline is about where it was in 1970. But since the rebirth of the inner city seemed to be directly related to the cost of energy and now that it once again cheap, did that mean that the inner cities and the suburbs would once again reverse roles? Are the suburbs now competitive again? Is it time for Jennifer and me to sell our houses that are located in walking distance of the downtown part of Charlottesville? The price of energy only dropped with the last year and we are already seeing a significant increase in auto traffic; sales of low mileage cars have increased, the sales of huge pickup trucks are on the rise and manufacturers are offering discounts when selling their new hybrid models. The love for the city may soon be over and once again people will prefer the suburbs. I am looking for the signs of what is happening and it is hard to tell. From my experience when living on Swann Street, there is a three year lag between a major shift in the price of energy and when it starts affecting the price of real estate.

Recent reports from the Washington DC area indicate that the city is losing residents. But it is not clear as to why this is happening. When a rundown section of a city starts to come back and a number of houses are renovated, there will be a movement of people out of that section. An old house that was converted years ago to two or three apartments where eight or ten people lived, when renovated back to being a single family house with only two or three people living there, this makes a loss of people in the area. Yet the real estate value will be much higher, tax revenue will grow and the new families will not require any social services as the poorer folks did who lived there before. Interestingly, while this is happening the number of cars on the street will significantly increase because the well-off family of three people may have three cars versus only one car or no cars when it was apartments.

In addition, once a neighborhood starts to come back and the real estate values increase the local developers will rise to the occasion and build high density housing such as condos and apartments. Then the population will increase and the number of cars on the street will skyrocket. When I first moved to Swann Street there were always a number of children playing in the street and there were plenty of street parking places. By the time I moved out the children were gone and street parking was hard to find. Therefore, whenever I read a report that suggests people are leaving the Washington DC area it is more a question of who is leaving and who is moving in. The same thing is happening in Charlottesville. Overall people are moving out. Some are poor and they are finding places in the county to live. Yet some people who are not poor and who moved into the city and lived there for a number of years ago are moving out. Maybe they are moving out for the same reason that I did about ten years ago when moving out of Arlington. It was because living there over the years, as the metropolitan area expanded, became part of the inner city. It grew so fast and so much that it became a hectic and confusing place to live. There was a lot of traffic and though I could walk to the office, if we wanted to go someplace there was always the issue of whether we could get there without massive traffic jams or whether there would be parking. The restaurants we went to depended on these two factors. When we first moved to Arlington and later to Charlottesville we found we could get anywhere in ten minutes and parking was not an issue.

It is the same in Belmont. Next to the Lyman Street lot that the developer wanted to rezone is the Belmont Lofts. It is a nice four story condo development with a number of penthouse apartments. There are 70 units and they are all middle income families. In the back of our house and across from Holly Street is a huge three acre lot where there are plans to build housing for senior citizens with over 300 units.

          STANTON BRAVERMAN

All over Belmont there is renovation of old homes, building of new homes on empty lots; new restaurants are coming in. At this point the population of autos in the area is increasing and along with it comes the traffic jams and the lack of parking spaces.

At the time we decided to come here the decision made sense. But if I had to do it again, knowing how backward the city governments in smaller cities can be, I probably would have decided to stay in Arlington. Now, after being here for years, there has been a huge increase in traffic as many people have moved in. The city does not have a well-run public transportation system which means most people have no choice but to go about their day to day lives driving a car. When they come into the downtown section they face a difficult parking situation. So being downtown has a lot of minuses and given the fact that the area is so spread out they can reach the far suburbs in a half -hour or less. When I lived in Rockville and worked a block from the White House it often took an hour and a half to get to work. It was a highly stressful experience and when the choice was to live on Swann Street versus spending hours each week wasting my life as I just sat in a car in a traffic jam, the choice of moving into the city made a lot of sense. But that was in 1972. Today the world is different.

Many government agencies that used to be in the city have moved out to other places. They did this because of political pressure and the need to find affordable housing for the staff. Houses in Culpeper, where a couple of government agencies are opening offices, are at least half the cost of the same house within the beltway.

Then there is the phenomenon of people working at home, sometimes on a full time basis and other times on a part time basis. They do not need to be facing the traffic crunch of the bigger cities on a daily basis or, they may never have to make the trip.

I was walking with Kodie the other night and saw a couple of young men loading up a truck with their furniture and things. I asked where they are going and they said "Waynesboro," which is a small town about 25 miles outside of Charlottesville. I asked why and they said that the cost of housing there was half the price. They pointed out that the daily commute to their jobs in the city was less than a half hour. "We love the city, but we use do not use the local businesses on a regular basis. Besides most of the movie houses have closed, there is only one left and it borders the city at the suburbs. There is less crime and lots of people our age." To them, it was time to go, especially now that the price of gasoline is low and the cost of getting back and forth to work is not expensive. They also pointed out one more thing: they carpool into work so they make the trip together. They figured it all out and they were right. Housing in Belmont has gotten very expensive and many of the young families that saw it as a nice place to buy a house at a decent price are no longer coming around. The ones that are coming now are financially much better off. They have to be if they are buying a house for $500,000 that used to sell for $150,000. But then the question is whether there are enough people with this level of income who want to move into Belmont? Maybe one of them will buy my house at a nice price and I will once again move back to the cabin on a full time basis? And there is the question as to whether they will stay in the neighborhood when they realize the City Council does not care about them.

The inner city has another factor to deal with and that is the rise of the new shopping centers. They are not malls like they were years ago, but designed to be community centers. In the center is the shopping areas and they are surrounded by various types of housing. This concept was first implemented in Reston, Virginia. It was miles outside of town and difficult to reach. Real estate prices took a significant fall during the housing crisis. But today it has bounced back especially after the metro subway system reached them. If you live in or near Reston you have everything inner city life can offer without the huge traffic jams and at a lower price. It will not be the charming old buildings that exist in the older part of the larger cities. But the architecture will be attractive.

Recently I had to go to Richmond and on the way back decided to stop off at the ACAC health club. I am a member but use the facilities in downtown Charlottesville. The club there is located in Short Pump which 25 years ago was just farms. Today it is huge with massive amounts of shopping, trendy restaurants. Intermingled with this shopping is a significant number of residential housing. A lot of it

     STANTON BRAVERMAN

is townhouses and condo style apartments. It looked like a nice place to live. Everything is within walking distance or a bike ride. There is a Whole Foods store, A Trader Joe's, Walmart, Lowes, Home Depot and upscale department stores. A person who lived and worked in the area would not need an auto. A bicycle would do. These new shopping areas will soon compete with not only Belmont but all of Charlottesville. If the city government continues with its haughty attitude they will soon find that the world has left them behind.

But other trends are affecting the situation. Within inner city there is not actually that much residential housing. Most of it is located within the surrounding suburbs. It will not take a huge increase in the number of people who want to move closer in to keep housing prices at their current level.

And then there is the issue that in spite of the interests in the surrounding county to keep the poor confined in the city, there has been a significant migration of poor people to the suburbs. And many suburban sections are becoming the ghettos of the future. Over the last ten years there has been a slow but steady increase in the number of families living at the poverty level that are now in the suburban areas. The reason for this trend is the fact that developers twenty years ago built lovely garden apartments in the suburban areas. Over the years these apartment buildings that were often built with cheap materials are quickly decaying and the original families that lived there have moved on to other communities. In addition, with the return of the middle class to the inner cities the cost of housing in the city has increased and the poor no longer can afford it.As the housing prices in the city increase and as the social services needs of the county also increase, maybe the country will want to merge with the city. They will find an increase in revenue that can be used to meet their needs.

The question is whether this trend will continue and it probably will because there are a lot of developments in the suburbs that were built years ago that are decaying and their cost is coming down.

There is another aspect of this situation that makes any prediction very difficult and that is the cost of transportation. The automobile is the most efficient transportation system so long as there are more than two people in the car. And while some academics do not understand how this works, the average American family does. To observe it, take a ride on the nearest interstate at the beginning of a major holiday when families are on the road to visit relatives. It can be Christmas, or July 4th or Labor Day or any weekend during the summer. The highway will be packed with minivans fully loaded with families. There will be four or more people in the van. The cost of transportation for four people going from Washington DC to Disney World in Orlando Florida in a car and stopping at night at a motel is a lot cheaper than airline tickets. Most American families have two cars. One is a gas efficient car and the other will consume a lot of gas. The efficient car is to be used to get around town and the gas guzzler is for family trips.

During the first energy crisis, Richard Nixon was president. I do not know if many readers remember him. He was known as "Tricky Dick" by upcoming liberals such as me. His administration was actually very creative in dealing with the crisis. They encouraged van pools. If a person bought a van that could take eight or ten people into the city at a time, they would give the operator a tax break and free parking space. It worked great. Every morning on interstate 95 going into the city were massive numbers of vans. With a lot of cars off the road they could move quickly. The demand for gasoline sharply declined and it helped to end the crisis. I do not know why the program ended or was not reinstated when a subsequent energy crisis happened. I suspect that the petroleum industry did not like what happened and has lobbied the government to find other ways of dealing with the energy crisis.

Eddie Summers, who was then an associate in my office, told me that there was an interesting seminar at the university that I should attend. It was given by a professor who had a grant to study why Manassas, Virginia went crazy when a massive number of Latinos moved into the county. It dealt with an immigration issue which was of interest to me. I went to the seminar and quickly realized the Economic professor just did not get it right. He was far off base. The first thing he did was to tell everyone that at that time there was a massive influx of Mexicans into the United States and that precipitated the problem. This was clearly an incorrect analysis because first, most of the Latinos

     STANTON BRAVERMAN

who moved into Manassas were from Central America – El Salvador, Guatemala and others. They were not Mexicans. Second, most of the Mexicans are not living in the Washington DC metropolitan area. They stayed in the smaller rural communities and in farm communities. Therefore the increase in Mexican illegal immigration was not causing the migration of Latinos from Central America to Manassas.

The second part of his presentation was a study of each of the surrounding counties regarding the increase in the number of Latinos living there. And it showed rather large increases in the numbers living in all counties except one and that was Arlington County, where there was a serious drop in the number of Latinos living there. The professor giving the lecture stated that he could not understand why Arlington was different and just ignored it as an anomaly. I listened to this conclusion and quickly raised my hand.

"There is a clear reason for the sudden drop off in Latinos in Arlington County. I saw it with my own eyes because I lived there and my office was there. The reason they left is because there was a sudden and steep increase in the price of real estate in the county and they could no longer afford to live there. Most of them were from Central America, many of them were my clients, and they all moved to Manassas." They did not move because a huge number of Mexicans showed up, they moved because they could not afford to stay. The reason why they chose Manassas was because they could afford to live there due of its close proximity to Interstate 66, which allowed for them to carpool, get in the HOV lanes and quickly get into the city where most of them worked at construction jobs. They had learned that a van, or truck or car that is fully loaded with passengers is a highly efficient way to travel. Again I often personally observed this. When I lived in Arlington and at times after work would go the mountain cabin, I found myself sitting in a massive traffic jam of cars with only one passenger and I would look over to the HOV lane and see the immigrants smoothly going by. At that moment I realized that maybe they were smarter than I was.

Historically, the poor were better off living in the city. That is where the jobs were and that is where they could find affordable housing. In the 1970's when I moved into Swann Street and saw the poor neighbors moving out I wondered if I was not participating in a movement where urban renewal was Negro removal. About half the families did not own the house they lived in and when the owner sold the house to a yuppie from the suburbs I was concerned about where they would go. Soon I realized that they were moving into the neighborhoods where the yuppie came from. In effect they were changing places. The living conditions for them in the suburbs were often far better than the condition of the rental house down the block. The local schools for the children were better and it seemed to be good moves for everyone. At the same time Mayor Barry was able to increase the city revenue which he used to provide needed social programs for the poor folk who stayed behind. One African American woman who was an officer at the local Immigration Office, who I would argue with about a client's application one moment and then see her at the local lunch counter the next where we would talk about our families, got upset when she learned that I moved into Swann Street. "Stan, when us Black folk were pushing for integration we were not talking about our neighborhoods. We were talking about the white folk neighborhoods." Then two years later she came up to me and said, "Guess what happened to the block where I live?"

"OK let me guess. A white man moved into the neighborhood."

"You got it. They are real nice and everyone is excited that they are there."

But today, the situation has drastically changed and it is doubtful if many of the poor want to return to the inner city. They are comfortable in the suburbs and they know that, by ride sharing, they have a highly efficient transportation system. Besides the old dilapidated old house that they left behind is now too expensive for them.

Put all of this together and we see that the inner city could be facing serious competition. Life is coming back to the suburbs and people are moving there because lower energy prices, HOV lanes and carpooling, it is affordable. In addition the inner city has to compete with the new wave of shopping centers and the surrounding housing they have built. Add to this, a refusal of the City Council to face the reality of the situation, and to continue to ignore its own people and once again it

      STANTON BRAVERMAN

looks like the inner city will fade away. They can compete, but they do not know how to compete. They are stuck on the advice they get from developers who will go by trends and often understand these population trends too late. When the developers see the trend going back to the suburbs they will quickly give up on the inner city and the best friend that the City Council had will be gone.

The developers overbuilt homes in the suburbs. Now they are overbuilding residential housing in the cities. They have a "monkey see, monkey do" attitude toward where they will build. If one builder is successful with an inner city project they will rush there to do likewise. If one builder returns to the suburbs and is successful they will return to that housing market. Unless the city and county councils take charge over neighborhood planning they will only add to the chaos.

CHAPTER 28

WHERE DOES URBAN RENEWAL GO FROM HERE?

THERE SEEMS TO be a slow and steady migration of Yankees to Southern states. They are leaving the Northern parts of the country for a number of reasons. But this all focuses around one aspect of life in the North. And that fact is its infrastructure and community relationships are old and outdated. They rely heavily on automobile transportation where there is one, at times, maybe two people to a car. The roads are congested; their bridges are old and need of repair which makes life there very difficult. Many of them talk about getting out of the area if they get a chance. They have heard from friends that life in the South is more comfortable and the cost of living is a lot cheaper. They are enticed to sell their houses in the North for a lot of money and then head south where they can buy a house for a lot less. Often the Southern city they go to is glad to get the new residents. They have what every small town wants and that is money. But the local government does not know how to deal with the expanding population. They will not invest in roads or public transportation; they do not understand what the new residents expect from living in a Southern town. Soon, the numbers of residents grow and slowly the city starts to be a miniature of what the Yankees left behind - traffic jams and inadequate public transportation. While this is happening and until the city reaches its saturation point the local government is cocky that they have everything people want and it will go on forever. But one day the city council and the developers wake up and realize that the roads are too crowded, the cost of housing has gotten too high and the Yankees stop coming. This has happened in Fredericksburg VA, Savannah Georgia and Charleston

South Carolina and it will soon happen in Charlottesville. Often when friends from Northern Virginia visit us they are shocked at the amount of traffic on route 29 as it approaches the inner city. The rush hour traffic slowly increases. It used to start at 5:00 when the hospital and university staff leave and return home and be over with by 5:30. But now it goes on until six. The backup at the Ruckersville light used to clear up very fast and now goes on longer as more and more cars head to the area. The city needs a bypass around the city but too many people opposed the idea and instead have supported a huge project to widen a street that has already been widened to four lanes on each side. The project will take at least two years and will adversely affect almost all of the businesses on that section of route 29. It is the main route for UVA football games which brings into town about 60,000 people. I do not know how they will get through the construction. The original proposal was a bypass around the town but the only way it could go would be through some large estates owned by a number of very rich people. The county believes that the suburbs will continue to grow and people will move there so long as they can get some access to the inner city. Route 29 will turn into a highway through the city that will allow for people to work in the city and then get in their cars and drive to their homes in the suburbs.

This is exactly the urban planning that was done in Detroit that in the end left the city with a very large population of poor families, which was a huge social cost burden to whomever remained; this caused the city to go bankrupt. The original game plan for that city was to keep all the poor inside the city and have everyone else live in the suburbs.

And that is what they are planning for Charlottesville. Va. The city just completed the John Warner Highway which takes traffic from the downtown area and channels it to route 29 and then on to the suburbs. The highway or parkway as they call it is already close to the maximum amount of traffic it can handle and it only opened a few months ago. Soon this highway will need to be expanded but no one knows where the money will come from. At the same time the City Council is talking about building additional bridges that are not for the people who reside in the city but to allow more people to escape the city for the suburbs.

The one bridge that ties the city together, the Belmont Bridge, is in serious need for repair, But the City Council will not provide funds for its construction and they believe they can appease the community by paying lots of money to bridge design companies who hopefully, once they get paid, will lose the plans. At the same time there is a massive amount of residential housing currently going up in the city with the expectation that thousands of more people will move there. These houses are built very close together with minimum parking space. As a result city planning seems to be going in two different directions at once. They are allowing the inner city to be built up with many new homes and almost no parking spaces and at the same time they are designing road structures to quickly get people out of the city. But no one has thought about how they will handle the traffic that will arise if they actually get that many people to move there. The one thing that is missing in small towns such as Charlottesville is mass transportation systems. There is a bus service that provides some inner city travel but it is not well developed and as a result most people who live in the inner city still need a car to get to work and for shopping.

But there is another obstacle to getting a decent highway system and mass transit system built in the US. And that obstacle is money. The country is broke, not as bad as Detroit but it just does not have the money to do very much. There has been some discussion in the news about the economic meltdown in Greece and the need for a number of serious economic reforms. Pensions may have to be cut, the government will have to follow an aggressive tax collection policy, and there is a need to cut the number of holidays and some other social benefits. But many economists rebut the notion that the US may be close behind Greece and they make this analysis with an item by item analysis. Most US pensions are financially sound for the moment though a few years ago they were in poor financial condition which meant that many pension benefits were significantly cut. The US does not need an aggressive tax collection policy though a number of tax experts claim that the primary reason for the US budget deficit is that too many Americans are cheating on their tax returns and the government just does not have the manpower at the moment to go after them. And if you talk to

          STANTON BRAVERMAN

people and look at the statistics that the government cites all the time, it appears that the country is rich. So where is the money? The answer is that it is in two places. First, there is a lot of money with the rich in that they have huge amounts of cash and other assets which are not available to most of the country. There are many articles in the news that the statistics show about 2% of the people own 90% of the wealth. These people, when they act collectively are powerful and are capable of keeping taxes on their wealth at low levels. Many people suggest that they be taxed but the rich have been putting together one scheme after another for hundreds of years to avoid paying taxes. They would rather pay a tax accountant a lot of money to find a way to avoid paying taxes versus paying a tax. In law school I found subjects such as corporate law, property law, and tax law to focus on one attempt after another by the rich to avoid paying taxes. It is reflected in our concepts of property law which go back to the 13th century. Taxing the rich is like shadow boxing. You seldom can impose a tax on the rich for the long term. They will find a way to get rid of it. The problem today is that a few people are so fantastically rich that it has the US economy out of balance, because they are not interested in spending or investing it.

Then there is another problem and that is what people call Crony Capitalism. This exists when the government for one reason or another decides to pass regulation or to subsidize one sector of the economy. Officially the government claims it is done for the public good but many people will question the truth of that concept. Almost every industry in the US has gotten some benefit from the government to neutralize any threat of competition. While these benefits are a form of corruption of the free enterprise system that conceptually is the keystone to our economy, Crony Capitalism has been around since the early days of the industrial revolution. In the time of Shakespeare the monarchy passed a law that all commoners had to wear a wool cap when they were outside. It was officially done to protect the people from colds but in reality it was imposed as a way to help out the newly organized textile factories where the primary ingredient they worked with was wool. Getting rid of crony capitalism is similar to imposing taxes on the rich, it is ingrained in our world and we have learned to live with it.

In effect, the economic system is interplay between the rich avoiding taxes and the business community getting benefits from the government, with what is left over going to the rest of the population. You may say that they pick up the crumbs; in more sophisticated language, it's called trickle- down economics. Hopefully there is enough to trickle down that the population is able to support itself and for the economy to be internationally competitive. In a strange way, the economy is like a washing machine. Money is the soap that cleans up everything and it goes from one corner of the economy to another and then back again. When a company hires employees it pays them a salary. The employees use that money to buy things they need. Sooner or later it goes back to the originating company who then spends some of the money once again to pay salaries. In effect, the money is supposed to spin around the system. And like a washing machine, it can go out of balance. Everyone who has ever used a washing machine knows what it is like when it is out of balance. The machine will jump around all over the place, it will make a loud noise and it is clear that if something is not done the machine will shake apart. In order to deal with the problem it is necessary to turn it off, open up the door and shift the clothes around to make it spin more smoothly. Washing machines, when running, are not perfectly balanced. They can take a lot of the load while being off balance. All of this is true with the economy as it spins around. We can handle a certain amount of crony stuff but when it gets too large the system goes out of balance too much then it will let you know that something has to be done.

Again, I go back to the analogy of the washing machine. There is no set recipe for when it goes out of balance. It is not just a pile of dirty underwear that will do it, or just a load of towels. Each load has its own balancing issues as each economy has its own crony capitalism issues. In Greece the imbalance appears to be the result of too many social services that the country cannot afford. And in the US the one piece of laundry that has spun the US system out of balance is healthcare. At the present time the healthcare costs in the United States is approaching 20% of Gross Domestic Product. That means that for every dollar spent in the country in one year, 20 cents is for healthcare costs. Every other

 STANTON BRAVERMAN

developed country has advanced healthcare systems similar to the US but their costs are between 9% to 13% of GDP. On average it is about 11% of GDP. There is no reason why the US healthcare system should cost more than the other developed countries. We all produce similar products, we have similar wage costs and we all have free enterprise economies that are plagued with the rich refusing to pay taxes and many industries getting various types of support from the government. But the excessive healthcare costs in the US have seriously disrupted the system and as a result the system is out of balance.

In other developed countries the average life expectancy is about the same as the US, the hospitals are similar and the drugs they take are similar. Then why is the US consumer paying about twice the cost of consumers in other countries? Now, everyone will say at this point, "It is crony capitalism and it exists everywhere." And that is true. But the crony aspect of the equation shows it is far too much and it is keeping the rest of the economy from being productive. To understand this, the reader has to understand how large the waste is. Healthcare is a three trillion dollar a year industry of which about one third or more is wasted. That amounts to one trillion dollars a year; it comes out to $4000 a year per person. This is not the total cost per person. That amount would be $8500 a year per person. It is $4,000 of that amount that is wasted. For a family of four people, (father, mother and two children) it amounts to $16,000 a year. Over a ten year period the waste amounts to $160,000 and over a thirty year period of an employee's working career it amounts to about a half a million dollars. Now, once again, I must repeat, this is the money that is wasted.

This amount of money is huge. To give a person an idea as to the size of the waste, if we gave it to the military the US could triple its size. The US military is already the largest standing army in the world and the most expensive to run. Many Americans have been in the US armed forces and are well aware how big it is. It is almost impossible to imagine a need to triple its size. One friend laughed when I mentioned that the waste was of such a magnitude and he could not in any way visualize how big one trillion dollars was. I looked at him and said that if the US decided to use that money to build Nimitz Class Nuclear

Powered Aircraft carriers, the Navy would get each year somewhere between 70 to 80 new ships. At the present time the Navy only has eleven such ships.

Another way to visualize the size of the waste is to consider using the waste to pay off student loans that currently amount to about a trillion dollars. If we decided to do this we could pay off all student loans in about 15 months. That will allow millions of Americans to attend college to get the technical skills the country needs to survive. Instead, we require the student to apply for huge amounts of student loans that are a financial burden for many years. And now, as a result of the so called Affordable Care Act, which is at times referred to as the unaffordable care act, the student once he graduates has to purchase a health insurance policy at very high costs, even though some of it may be subsidized by the government.

It is amazing that older generation in America often wonder why the younger generation is not as active as they were and seem to be unconcerned about getting ahead. The reason is simple: the older generation did not get hit with expensive student loans and health insurance premiums were reasonable. Compare that today with a student who gets a Doctorate degree in physical therapy and ends up with $100,000 or more in student loans with an interest rate as high as 7% and a health insurance policy that costs another $300 a month. It is clear that the country does not want to invest in its youth and expects them to pay their way through student loans with high interest rates, healthcare costs that are unreasonable and pension programs that probably will fail before they retire. And yet we ask our youth to be positive forces in our economy. But a country that refuses to invest in its youth will find that the youth will not invest in it.

      STANTON BRAVERMAN

CHAPTER 29

THE FAILURE OF DATA ANALYSIS

B UT AMERICANS DO not seem to react to the abuses that are put on them. Maybe it is a result of the fact that they feel secure in their day to day lives or they somehow feel that the government and big business is really trying to deal with the problems. Maybe they need to be squeezed a lot more before they begin to react. The rich and the government have their arguments in place to fight back. They will focus on statistics and data. They will produce piles of them to justify what they want to do or they will claim that we need more statistics and data before we can make a decision. This is one result of computer technology and the ability of the machine to store and manipulate huge amounts of data. Recent mandatory changes in the US healthcare system call for collecting a huge amount of data. The prediction is that this will allow for the determination of various techniques that will lead the system to operate more efficiently. This has been the rallying call of Corporate America and the government for the last 75 years. For example, the tobacco companies fought back on controls over public smoking and increases in cigarette taxes for years by claiming that the database used in various studies was not big enough or that the statistical techniques were flawed. The lead industry did the same thing for years which allowed for most lead restrictions to be put off for many years. In both cases when most people knew of someone who died from smoking or knew of someone with lead poisoning and the need to correct the problem became obvious did the industry accept government controls. The same arguments now are heard with climate change and global warming. The storms are getting stronger, the sea level is rising and hurricanes have come close to closing down New York City. But the opponents claim that the data does not clearly show that this is related to the 100 million barrels of oil used each day in autos or the millions of coal trains that deliver coal to power plants. They claim that the data will show us the way. Yet the data is never clear enough for a respectable decision.

The same type of analysis is followed by the City Council that avoids making decisions by announcing a need to further study a problem even when the solution if obvious. There is a need for one more evaluation for a new bridge. How can it be done cheaper? Do we really need it? Can we put it off forever? They search for more statistics. The Zoning Board did not want to deny the rezoning of Lyman Street and announced that they needed to find old data and information. But when they want to make a decision then they overlook the data as when the mayor announced at the City Council meeting, "We heard enough, now let's vote," or when the Zoning Board in the back room announced that the application was approved without any concern for the underlying truth.

The search for data can be compared to the search for God. We believe the real answer is out there and forever we will search for it. And while many decent people in the world have an honest day to day search for God, there are many people who use the search as a basis for decisions that serve their own self-interests; data analysts function the same way. The economist at the seminar trusted his data but could not find the answer. He was honest at what he reported. But others are not this way.

Moreover, in recent years the data specialists have caused serious damage to our economy such as the collapse of the housing market a few years ago which almost forced the closure of most American banks. It all started with data analysis in the mortgage market. The loan companies would put into a large packet a number of mortgages they issued and would sell them to foreign banks. They did a statistical evaluation of the packets and concluded that the risk of loss, because of the large number of mortgages in each packet, would be so small that it would be considered as zero risk. This analysis was based on an algorithm that was the focus of many MBA degrees at business schools

     STANTON BRAVERMAN

all over the country. This type of analysis was attractive to the banks and investment funds that wanted to buy the bonds if they would be guaranteed by a respectable large size American bank. The US banks were willing to do this, but they had a problem and that was technically they could not use the word "guarantee." If they used the word guarantee they would have to show it on their financial statements and report them as contingent liabilities to the Bank Examiners. Since the algorithm and the data showed that there was zero risk in guaranteeing the bundle of mortgages they created a new word called "derivatives". The banks then in effect guaranteed the bonds, got a fee and since they were considered to have zero risk they did not even show them as contingent liabilities. However, these "derivatives" failed and the banks had to buy back the mortgages at the original price.

When I argue with data specialists about the limitations of data analysis they look at me and say. "Braverman, you are an attorney. What do you know about data?" And the answer is I know a lot. While at the Treasury I was considered a specialist in data analysis. Here was a 25 year old kid working on highly important stuff that at times would go to the Congress or to the White House. A senior official would call me to his office and ask if I could look into the statistics of some aspect of the international economy. I would then quietly close the door to the office and ask the official what he wanted the data to show. Once I knew what they were trying to achieve I would go to the Treasury library where there were statistical reports that went back for many years, spend time going through them and then preparing the chart. While the data was never false, I was skilled at manipulating the data to show what they wanted it to show. It was a simple exercise in the concept that "statistics do not lie, but liars use statistics."

One Saturday at Treasury, while working on what was an important table, an epiphany came to me that sent my life into a different direction. It was part of an important report that was to go to the President of the US dealing with the World Bank. There was a rush to get it done and it was late in the afternoon. The data led me down a road with a fork in it. I had to go in one direction or the other and needed to get the advice of my boss. I went to his office, but he was not there. He was in his boss's office. So I went there, but they were not there. They were in their boss's boss's office and I went there. But it turned out that everyone was in the Under Secretary of the Treasury's office discussing the same issue for which I needed an answer. And, because I was just a low level government employee, I was not allowed into this inner sanctuary. I was the expert on the issue, I knew it backwards and forwards, aspects of it that related to other government activities but I was outranked and sent back to my office. Since it was late and I was tired I went back to my office, locked up all the classified material and took the elevator to the basement. On Saturday the main door was locked and the only way out of the building was through the basement. At the last minute before leaving the building and realizing it was at least an hour's ride to Rockville I decided to go into the nearby men's room, which was used by the janitorial staff, to pee. There was graffiti written all over the walls. At the urinal I started to pee. In front on me the graffiti said, "Look up." I raised my head to look up only to see another sign that said, "Look up higher." I did that and my neck was stretched back as far as it could go and the sign said, "Look down, you are pissing on your shoes." How true it was! What a revelation. When I was a child at the treasury and spoke and worked like a child, I did childish things. The charts were childish and it was time for me to grow up. Soon I enrolled in law school, finished it at night on a part time basis and passed the bar exam in less than three and a half years. I left the Treasury and spent the rest of my life looking down and having little respect for people who stretched out their necks to look up.

In my suggestions for what to do with the savings from healthcare waste under a more efficient system, I talked of using the money to pay off student loans. Once all student loans are paid off we can start using the money for needed infrastructure such as new bridges, highways, mass transportation projects The Obama administration announced that it needed $60 billion for new bridges to repair the ones that are not safe. This amounts to about 6% of the waste each year in healthcare costs. If we used this amount of waste for bridges we would still have $900 + billion to spend or use to pay down the national debt. That means we can build our bridges and pay off all student loans in 18 months.

   STANTON BRAVERMAN

Many people claim that the other developed countries had socialist run healthcare systems and that means that it will allow the government to determine if you are going to live or die. This argument just does not make sense. It assumes the public can trust private enterprise to behave in a way that will want to keep them alive. But Corporate America never has a serious interest in keeping people alive. Their interests are in making money. To let corporate America decide whether a person can get the medical services they require is scary. It could easily turn into a situation where you are worth more to them if you are dead than alive. Currently they have more of an interest in seeing that the average person is unhealthy and in need of medical attention, which means they need health insurance rather than encouraging them to be healthy. It is corporate America that develops a pill for dealing with hepatitis C that costs $100,000 a year and they have little concern that if the patient lives or dies. They just want the money. Anthem, a major healthcare insurance company, recently announced that the healthcare system improved so much that only 400,000 people died that year from improper medical treatments at US hospitals. That figure shocked me since the same figure was reported to be 300.000 a year a few years earlier. It takes guts for a health insurer to brag about how well it is doing while it goes around killing more and more people and it takes a gullible American public to accept the statistic as showing an improvement in our lives. .

A number of people will claim that the US healthcare system will find a way to give everyone the medical attention they need. Yet everyone knows someone who cannot afford a doctor or afford drugs he/she needs and is not being taken care of. In addition, the Federal Government and the State governments provide a huge amount of money for healthcare through Medicare, Medicaid, and veterans' benefits. The cost of these programs amounts to about 45% of the total healthcare costs in the country.

Look closely at the statistics and they get even scarier. Of the total healthcare costs in the US of three trillion dollars a year, the 45% that is paid for by the Federal and State governments amounts to about $4000 a person (public and private contribution amounts to $8500 a person a year). This amount exceeds the amount that Canadian government pays for its socialist healthcare system. I spent an evening comparing the costs between the two systems and concluded that if the federal and the state governments took all the money they are currently paying for healthcare and channeled it into a Canadian style system the health insurance costs of every person would be $50 a month, there would be no co-payments, and it would include dental and eye care. Wow, are we getting screwed. We cannot afford bridges, we cannot afford to properly educate our youth, we are killing massive numbers of people each year and the cost of healthcare is expected to increase by 6% a year.

The whole system is nuts. One day the government says that cost increase will be 6% a year when they should be decreasing by this amount. Then when the public gets upset about this rate of cost increase the government announces that they re-evaluated the issue and determined that the cost increase will only be 3% a year and then a month later most of the health insurance companies announce that they will seek rate increases as high as 40% a year. The most recent propaganda from Washington is that health insurance will only increase by "only" 4% next year when it should be decreasing by this amount. What is amazing about the 6%, 4% or 3% increase in costs that the government portrays as being improvements is the amount of money it relates to. For a $3 trillion dollar a year system a 6% increase would cost both the government and the public $180 billion a year. At 4% it would cost $120 billion a year and at 3% it would cost only $60 billion a year. Anyone of these numbers is a huge amount of money.

What does all this information about healthcare have to do with the problems I have with my house on Douglas Avenue? The answer is that there is a strong connection. If there was money to build the bridge then the folks in Belmont will feel that they are part of the city. But the city claims it does not have the $16 million for the bridge. The state government does not have it and neither does the federal government. That means every time I cross the bridge I run a risk that it may just collapse on me. But there is never an argument or concern about the American public having to pay an additional $60 billion to $180 billion a year to maintain an overpriced healthcare system that is on the

                    STANTON BRAVERMAN

verge of collapse. To deal with the healthcare cost issue it would mean requiring the University of Virginia Hospital and healthcare operations to stop raising their costs. But the UVA system is very well connected and wants to keep the basic structure of the healthcare system in place.

But the university could benefit from an economically efficient healthcare system. If the waste in healthcare paid off student loans then more young adults could afford to get degrees. That would increase enrollment at the University of Virginia. It will allow for some increase in tuition rates. The increase in student enrollment in turn would increase the overall economic activity of the city. It is like a washing machine that is spinning around, only it would be more efficient and would be more in balance.

If the government had the money for expanding the interstate highways and could take the pressure off of Route 29 and it would not be necessary to close down the business district for two years for an underpass that is not needed.

Instead they leave the machine out of balance. And the sad part about it is that no one is willing to do anything about it and that is because there are not many people who still hear the words of John F. Kennedy or if they did, they got it backwards and are asking what the country can do for them. The City Council supported by the rich in the surrounding county with their $14 million a year feel exactly that way and their greed is what led to Douglas Street being ground zero. And until they realize that Belmont and all the citizens of the city are of equal standing they will continue to be my worst enemy.

To deal with this problem it is important that many new people move to the town. It is a great town and with their help it can be a better place to live. The city needs them to register to vote and to vote against the misdirected programs of the City Council. Move into Belmont, walk through the city center, eat at local restaurants and together we can make it be what we want it to be. When you are here for a while you can go to Jeff's garage and have your picture taken as many of the students do next to the artwork that says "I love Charlottesville a Lot" and you can post it on Facebook and tell them that you were a part of a new movement.

CHAPTER 30

FINAL COMMENTS

ONE MORE INTERESTING comment: In the fall of 2014, while I was at the mountain cabin, a strange man came up to visit with a neighbor. He said he was a film director and was looking for a site for part of a movie he was making. I did not like the man, and I still do not like the man. In addition I do not like performing artists because at times I represented them when they needed visas to come to the US. I told him he could not use the property for the film. The name of the movie was "Coming Through the Rye" which has something to do with the book "Catcher in the Rye" and J.D. Salinger who was the author. Later that day I mentioned the conversation with Jennifer. She Googled the title and found that Chris Cooper would be in it. She got excited about the movie because Chris Cooper was one of her favorite actors and would be working at her cabin. She emailed the director and invited him back to the house.

Catcher in the Rye is a popular book about a young man from an upper class family northern family who has to grow up. After being told he is being kicked out from the third or fourth boarding school he leaves before the school year but is not sure where to go. He is concerned about going home early because the family may realize he is in trouble again and he wonders through the streets and parks of New York City. This book is required reading by almost every high school student or freshman in America. Each year parents rush to used-book stores to pick up a copy for their teenage sons or daughters to read. When I read it years ago I found it dull and did not relate to me. After all I did not attend boarding school or leave home to go to college. Those people who did so were in a different world than the one I lived in and I was not impressed when the Director told me the movie was about the relationship between a young man from a boarding school and the author.

There is the feeling that J. D. Salinger was a recluse and a lot of the feelings and emotions expressed in the book related personally to him. But he lived away from people as if he was escaping or running away from something. The young man, the main character in the book, who gets kicked out of all the boarding schools, keeps pointing out that he finds the world upsetting because it is full of "phonies." The movie is about a young man who reads the book and relates to it so well that he writes an adaptation for a school play which he asks if they can perform at the school. He is told that because of copyright requirement he will need J.D.'s approval and it will never happen. The young man does not give up and sets out on a journey to find the author who is living as a recluse in a mountain cabin that looks similar to the my cabin.

There were four days of filming, sixty people running all over the property. The living room became the computer center; the family room became the make-up room. The bedrooms and the guest cabin became the "green rooms" for the lead actors. The back lawn area was where they served lunch. I hung around the house and found that there were a lot of things I needed to help them with and I watched how a movie was made. After the production group left I found a copy of the book and reread it. This time I understood it. Holfield was right. He was from a haughty community where it was important to look good. It was important that a person act as though they were important. To do that, they had to be something other than themselves. In effect they were phonies. It was not important for the world to know who you really are. That stuff is only for your therapist or the favorite bartender to know. After rereading the book, I began to understand an aspect of my current personality and that is my dislike and distrust for the phonies of the world.

People at times ask me why I do not join mainstream society. That means giving up the rusted pickup for a BMW, joining a country club, buying clothes from a stylish shop and traveling around with the more elite crowd. The answer is "done that in the past and did not like it." While an Economist at the Treasury I attended functions at the White

House, at Embassies and various elite clubs in the area. I had many lunches with senior partners of major law firms. Whenever I was at these places I found I could not tell the real people from the phonies. Jennifer's family is in that world and when we are with them it is almost impossible to see where the fantasy ends and reality begins. This is to be contrasted with my youth in growing up in a Jewish ghetto in Philadelphia where everyone knew everything about you. They knew if you were rich or poor, or if you were a truck driver with a group of Teamsters, or living on Swann Street or Douglas Avenue when there were only poor people. Poor people generally do not have time to be something they are not. They have to be themselves to survive. There was the experience at the law firm where one's partner's intelligence extended only to his handshake. He could do that well and make you feel he maybe someone who is important. But it did not take long before it became clear that the man had very little to offer in the way of legal skills. It was the same when I faced off against the many lawyers at the hearing for Ragged Mountain. These lawyers' legal skills were haughtiness and intimidation. This does not meant that they were not good lawyers, but they did not present that side of themselves to me during the litigation.

That explains why I left Swann Street after it became an established community and why Belmont is no longer as exciting to me as when we first got the house. The so-called upper class that moved in is more difficult to understand and I prefer not to be there. There is my refuge in the mountains where a recluse such as J.D could go to hide and think.

In a couple of weeks the movie which was filmed at the cabin will premiere at the Virginia Film Festival in Charlottesville. Jennifer bought a number of tickets and I am supposed to go. It means leaving the comfort of the mountain cabin and going into the land of the phonies and seeing a play about a young man who started to see the reality of the world, given by a Director who likes to tell the people in phony land a story about themselves, the real message of which will pass over them. After all, they are and will be seen at the film festival and that alone will impress most people.

CHAPTER 31

UPDATE

WRITER'S NOTE: THIS is the end of the book as originally written. It was done a few years ago and then put away along with other unfinished books. At times I would send a copy to a friend and they would be after me to finish it and have it published. I was reluctant to do it because it meant that I would have to face criticism from many people. The feeling is similar to the anxiety an artist feels when completing a picture. However, one friend pushed hard to get me to edit it and get it published. While at the cabin one spring morning, looking out at the mountain, hearing the water cascade down the stream and the solitude that allows for clear thinking I agreed to do so. But there is more to say. The story about the Ragged Mountain Dam may seem incomplete. I deliberately left it that way and it is explained in the next part.

I am now back at writing and this time I know where I am - it is at the cabin, tucked away in a hidden corner of the Shenandoah Mountains, away from the chaos of Charlottesville. The war with the City Council is behind me and life here is easier to deal with. The locals work together to make the best of their lives. There are no contractors trying to uproot the neighborhood and no outlandish promises by petty politicians. The major turn of events that led to this change in life was Jennifer's long illness and her death. It was a devastating event that shook the purpose of my life to its core. Jennifer was my best friend, lover, companion, and adviser. Going on in life without her seemed to be impossible.

It all started with the diagnosis of pancreatic cancer. It stymied us and the world stopped moving. It took close to three years from the time of the diagnosis to her death. At times we felt that she won the fight and she would go on with her life. The blood tests were normal. But it came back. Slowly at first and then quickly it all ended. During this period the war with the Council was put aside and I had a need to find myself and figure out how to move on.

At that time we were basically living in two houses: one in the city and the other in the mountains. It was an hour drive between them. Many times one of us would spend the day at the cabin and return to the city at night. Other times we would spend the day in the city and then return to our home in the mountains. We were established locals and neighbors in both communities. But this arrangement could only be done while the two of us worked at it. Without Jennifer it was difficult to run both households. It became necessary to give up one of the two residences.

This was not an easy decision. I was 77 years old and did not have the energy to do the hard work that was required to maintain 30 acres, two houses (the main cabin and the guest cabin) plus pond work and vegetable garden. The property is miles away from a hospital or a doctor's office. There were a few neighbors, but no one that close to go to in an emergency. The city house was close to medical services and my daughter and grandchildren. At times I thought it would be best to rent out the mountain house.

But the other side of the equation was that life in the mountains is more relaxing; there is a lot of support from neighbors, though they are not around the corner. The issue of medical services was downgraded because I have a strong distrust of all doctors and felt that any treatment they gave to me when I was old would quicken my death. I thought of the old doctor who in his late 70's moved out to the next hollow to die from cancer. Instead he went on living for another 20 years. And there was clearly a medical benefit to country living on the blood pressure. There was a part of me that wanted to go back and fight "the Bastards" and another part said that the fight and the higher blood pressure would hasten my death. Maybe it was a fear of dying, or I knew the battle would go on and on no matter how many victories I had. Petty politicians will always be petty. But then again, maybe I just love living in the country – away from the madding crowd.

     STANTON BRAVERMAN

A lot of work was required in closing out the house in Charlottesville. There were two sets of everything – dishes, pots and pans, towels, clothing, furniture and cars. It took months to make the move. There were too many items that reflected our life together and getting rid of them was done piece by piece. The children got some of the furniture. Jennifer's clothes were given away to neighbors and thrift shops. Taking down family pictures that had been up for many years was the most difficult. There was a picture of cows in a river which Jennifer drew; it was based on a photo that Danny took when camping along the Shenandoah River. There was another of Kenny, Danny and me when they were about ten years old. It was the day we got the sailboat. I am at the stern looking out and they are curled up in my arms.

There were lots of food items in the refrigerator that Jennifer bought for herself. As I took them out to give away I felt that I was giving away part of her. As I cleaned out the drawers of the furniture I found many items that told me to hold on to them but I knew it was time to pass them on. But some I still have such as the match book that is from our wedding that says "Stan and Jennifer." The move went so slowly that some of my friends commented that I was not really planning on leaving the city. But the pace accelerated and soon it was the final move out day. The movers took what was left to the cabin, the house was now vacant and a "For Rent" sign was posted. Before I left I looked back and walked through the rooms. There was the bedroom where we would listen to the customers at the local restaurants telling everyone they loved them; there was the sound of the trains. Then in the living room the gas stove that looked like a wood stove that Jennifer would sit near on cold mornings drinking her first cup of coffee. I guessed it was the mountain house that saved me because Jennifer had many of her things there as well as in the city. After 40 years of living with someone it is impossible to just walk away and not reminisce about our life together.

There was the need to notify the bank, the government, the insurance companies and what seemed to be hundreds of other people and organizations of the change in address. Yet in my mind the move was not complete until one simple event took place. It was putting up a mailbox. We had the house for over 25 years and did not have a mailbox.

Life in the country is so simple that a mailbox was not necessary. For the first 15 years the mail went to the local post office. The street by the property did not have a name, there was no house number. Just my name at General Delivery, Syria, VA. One friend sent a letter to us addressed to Megan's Mom and it got to our post office box. After the attack on the World Trade Center and a nationwide campaign to make the country more secure the county named the road and assigned address numbers. But the cabin was so far back into the mountains that the post office refused to deliver mail and once again the mailing address was "General Delivery."

About four years ago, another house was built down the dirt road. That was the fourth house on the road and the emergency preparedness program required that there be a name to the dirt road -and a number for each house. I got a new address but still the post office refused to deliver mail here, which meant a five mile drive to get the mail. But then there was one other problem. The post office realized that they did not need to keep the local office open all day and limited the hours to two hours a day. At first this was still not an issue because all of the important mail was delivered to our house in Charlottesville. Now that the house in the town has been vacated there was a need for a more reliable way of getting mail and that would be a mailbox. I was then advised to go down the mountain to the end of the delivery line and put up a mailbox. There were already four boxes down there for the locals who lived near me.

I bought the post for the mailbox and got a metal box to fit on top. The postal clerk told me that there were a lot of regulations I should review before putting up the box. It had to be of a certain size, it could not be too far off the road and the numbers and letters should allow the delivery clerk to quickly know who the box relates to. Being a lawyer and fully away of the role of regulations I looked for them and could not find them anywhere. I just went to the end of the delivery route, dug a hole about as deep as the box next to me, jammed rocks in the hole to tighten up the pole and then attached the box and put the numbers to the house. Then I waited. The next day I went down the road with the "side by side" to see if there was mail and it was empty. The next day

     STANTON BRAVERMAN

it was the same. On the third day, I was returning home and pulled over to check - and there it was: one piece of mail. That event made me feel more secure than anything else I had done in that neighborhood. I could tell all the locals "See, I have a mailbox just as you do."

At times the world appears to be standing still and things will remain as they are forever. But that is an illusion and where we live today will not be that way for long. Swann Street, St Michaels, Arlington VA and Madison county and other neighborhoods where I have lived are not what they were fifty years ago. During the three years since Jennifer's death life has changed in Charlottesville and there is a need to update parts of this book. Belmont, because it is a comeback neighborhood, is changing. Old houses are being restored, new businesses are opening, old neighbors are moving out and new ones are moving in, but one thing has not changed: the need to go to war against the City Council.

In 2005 the assessed value of my house on Douglas Ave was $130,000. Today it is over $500,000. In 2005 there were a significant number of poor people who lived in the neighborhood. Today there are fewer poor people, a large number of middle income families and some rich families. In 2005 Belmont was a financial drain to the city that was trying to meet the needs of the poor. Today Belmont is a major source of revenue. Yet the city has not made any investment in the neighborhood and most of the increase appears to be going to updating and improving the facilities surrounding the university and the university hospital.

Adam did finally open his new restaurant, "The Junction", though most of us see it as not being a great place to go for dinner. La Taza has closed, and we were advised that the buyer was from Richmond Virginia. A new restaurant will soon open. Tomas, the Chef at Mas is no longer there. Instead he opened a restaurant where Spudnuts was located. It is no longer a Spudnuts. Many more houses on Douglas Street, Goodman and other streets have been renovated – one house, after renovation sold for almost $1 million. A number of lots have been turned over to developers.

Ian, after ten years of working on the Southern Crescent (and constant harassment from me that he made serious misrepresentation to the city to get the zoning change) finally opened. Most of the restoration of the old building was done by him. When it opened and I went inside I was flabbergasted to see how nice it looked. I had no choice but to publicly apologize to him and compliment him for a job well done.

One interesting change is the acceptance of taco trucks that serve a variety of gourmet foods. Some of them are sponsored by the local restaurants and go to events serving great food.

The bridge across the railroad tracks that connect the neighborhood with Charlottesville is still in need of repair. There is a sign on the bridge telling people who cross to think about a new bridge. Yet funds for a new bridge have yet to be appropriated and every year the City Council puts the cost of a new bridge into the budget and every year nothing happens. And the duct tape and bubble gum that is holding up the bridge seems to increase. A new consulting contract has been approved by the Council that will include a study of how to renovate the bridge - that has to come down.

Probably everyone is aware of the riots in the city between the Alt-right and the left and the death of Heather Heyer as a result of a terrorist attack on a peaceful demonstration. There were reports that the City Police Department just stood by while the riots occurred. While I was there to see the police lined up and ready to attack one side or the other they actually did nothing to stop the chaos. I saw a long procession of Alt-right protestors carrying Nazi symbols, clubs and other items that could be considered to be weapons as they marched right past the police and on to Lee Park where the statute of Robert E. Lee stood. Then the two groups met at various places in the downtown section and they turned the town into a war zone. Being a local and being so close to the events I have my own understanding of what happened. At that time there was only one African American who was on the Council. He was a relatively newcomer to the town. A teacher, he held himself out as wanting to represent both the African American and the White community. However, once he got to the Council his concept of racial harmony was to take down the statute of Robert E. Lee who was the leading general of the Confederate States during the Civil War (1869 to 1865.) A resolution in favor of taking down the statute was approved by the Council after a considerable amount of bargaining by the council

                    STANTON BRAVERMAN

members. Bob Fenwick stated that he voted for removing the statute as part of a political compromise where he wanted a number of proposed budget items that were to assist poorer families.

Most of the African Americans I talked to about the statute compared it to beating a dead horse. The Civil War was over 150 years ago, it was just a statute and the money spent on taking it down could be spent on other things the community needed. Some of them saw it as a "cheap shot" by the Council to convince the poor African Americans who lived in the city that something was being done to improve their living conditions.

Neither side expected any confrontation or riot as a result of the decision. But the Alt-right were feeling empowered and were trying to emerge as a political force. This was their chance to make headlines in the news. The Alt-left consisted of a number of members of the "occupy" movement that a few years before was active in the city and had taken over Lee Park. They camped out there for a long time and they often taunted the police. It seemed as if the Alt-right and the Alt-left were looking for a fight. Both sides held rallies. The police did not like either side, they felt that if they want to beat each other up, let them do so.

Racial relations in the town are still in need of significant improvement and two African Americans are now on the Council and working to get the city to spend more money on affordable housing. This new attitude toward affordable housing is pragmatic decision. The massive urbanization of poor neighborhoods has created a serious housing shortage for the poor folks in town, most of whom are African Americans. They are slowly being pushed out of their neighborhoods and have no place to go. They have been going to Council meetings for over a year, pushing for, screaming about and being disorderly in their attempt to get this message through to the Council. The two African American council members are aware of this issue and always push a developer who needs a zoning change to commit some of the development for affordable units, but at best it would be an insufficient number of units.

Eventually the Council realized that if they did not allocate funds for affordable housing then there could be serious riots. The city is slowly recovering from the stigma created by the altercation between the Alt-Right and the Alt-Left regarding the Lee statute. Another headline of such chaos would clearly label the city as a place to stay away from. What is amazing is that the millions of dollars the city receives each year from the county should be going to build affordable housing; this money was originally agreed upon to keep the city from expanding into the county, which at the time, it had the right to do. Affordable housing would not be an issue in the city if these funds were used for this purpose.

Because of the significant number of development project and the significant number of people who moved into them there are now more traffic jams. It takes longer to get through the town and parking is more difficult. But no one on the Council seems to care. A developer is planning on building a project that will be 130 residential units plus 18,000 square feet of commercial space in the lot behind my house on Douglas Ave. All of the traffic will go on to Carlton Ave which is already crowded with cars and trucks. The street cannot handle cars going in both directions at once and drivers are always trying to pull over to the side to let other cars by them. It is not an area for such high density traffic. The developer insists that he has the right to build the project based on existing zoning regulations, but that is not clear and it his argument can easily be attacked. But no one in the city government is concerned.

Another developer, the one who got his project on Layman Street turned down because the narrow streets could not handle the traffic, has re-submitted his project to the city for zoning changes. It looks like this time it may get through. I recently found out that he reapplied for the dead project. One of the neighbors told me that it is happening because I have moved out of town and there is no one to take up where I left off.

The city is encouraging the construction of a number of hotels in the downtown area. My guess is that they want to encourage more conventions and large business gatherings to increase tourism. While it is a great idea it will only add to the downtown traffic issues.

 STANTON BRAVERMAN

The City Council just passed a small increase in the hotel tax and is planning on using the funds to support low cost housing. It is not clear how many units will be built and whether this will be effective in dealing with the housing crisis of the poor in the town. But it will not come close to the money from revenue sharing that should be going for their housing.

Recently while sitting on the porch to the cabin, I thought about the adventure of living in Belmont. And I started to get emotional – almost crying and laughing. Across the street was a beat up old house where four drunks lived and also Connie, who was an old lady trying to survive on her welfare check. Jennifer and I would worry about them and at times bring them food. Even though it would seem that such a house would be a sad place, actually they were rather content with their lives. But slowly they all died. Connie died of blood poisoning from the filth. One of the drunks fell asleep on a very cold night and froze to death and one seemed to just move on. Today the house is renovated and university students now live there.

Next door to me is where Leo lives. He is almost an institution in the city. Like me, he moved there because it was a cheap place to live. He is now retired and I often saw him walking to the Live Arts building where he worked. The Live Arts is an old theater that is used for amateur plays. A school will put on a play or a local theater group will do so. They are always short a volunteer actor and Leo will be commandeered to take up the part. He was the janitor, ticketmaster and part time actor.

Next door to Leo was a family that I would call trailer trash that raised pit bull dogs. They were so dysfunctional that they twice burned down the house. Sometime after the second fire they moved back to a very rural area of the surrounding county. Recently the house sold for over $500,000 to a young professional.

My other neighbor is the rental house that is owned by Janet Hatcher. Shirley, Hope and Kenny live there. Shirley is close to 80 years old and Hope and Kenny are also well into retirement age. While living there Kodie decided to make them his other family and would often get out of the yard, go to their front door and bark to get inside. He would spend the day there. Hope would then walk Kodie around the neighborhood telling everyone that he was her dog. Shirley would often bring him home. It was amazing to watch a dog bring so much life into their lives. When I moved to the cabin they were clearly upset and I had to promise to bring Kodie to them at least one day a week. The dog is not excited about living at the cabin. Life there is just too quiet for him. And when I yell out "Kodie, get in the car. We are going to Shirley's" he quickly jumps in – even though he dislikes car rides.

The list of characters in the neighborhood goes on. But most are gone and the new neighbors are nice people but to me not as exciting. As the theme of this book repeats, neighborhoods change, life goes on and all we have to show for it are memories.

However, as the developers build more residential units and as more people move into these areas there is slowly developing a new political force that the politicians and the developers have to deal with. One of the first questions a new resident asks after moving into town is "When are they going to stop all of this out of control development?" These people vote and they want their needs met. They did not move into the city to face increasing levels of city type confusion. This phenomena has already shown itself at neighborhood meetings where a large number of active residents want to stop development. One such example was with the project behind my house and the 160 units that is planned for. The developer originally wanted to include many more units which called for a zoning change. After seeing the outpouring of anger against the project by the current neighbors he reduced the plan to 160 and is arguing that he does not need a zoning change and can do it under the existing right he has. This claim is debatable but no one is prepared yet to challenge him.

The hope is that Charlottesville will follow the path of Arlington. In the 1960's, it was a redneck town that seemed to be run by the American Nazi Party. But over time, as Washington metropolitan area grew and many well educated professionals moved there, the city council got more enlightened and today it is probably a first class well run government. For a while I thought this was going to happen in Charlottesville. A new major, Mike Signer, was in office and he was raised in Arlington. But he got caught up in the chaos of the Alt-right and Alt-left riots

     STANTON BRAVERMAN

which stigmatized people's perception of him. Also, to me, Mike seemed to focus too much on supporting the developers at a time the local population was tired of them.

The one thing that Charlottesville does not yet have is the large number of professional residents who are willing to go to bat for the community. I was such a person and it worked but I could not do it alone. In the 1970s in Arlington a large number of professionals moved into the city and were active in city government. They were the ones who forced the city to adopt policies that benefited all of the community. Hopefully in Cville, as the developers build more housing for middle income families and as they immigrate to the city there is an expectation that there will be enough trouble makers such as me to do the job. There is a lot of potential in the city and the county. But it takes a large number of active people to take over the City Council to get the job done.